For the Love of
Chocolate

Karen Rowe

BLUE
BIKE
BOOKS

© 2008 by Blue Bike Books
First printed in 2008 10 9 8 7 6 5 4 3 2 1
Printed in Canada

All rights reserved. No part of this work covered by the copyrights
hereon may be reproduced or used in any form or by any means—
graphic, electronic or mechanical—without the prior written permission
of the publisher, except for reviewers, who may quote brief passages. Any
request for photocopying, recording, taping or storage on information
retrieval systems of any part of this work shall be directed in writing to
the publisher.

The Publisher: Blue Bike Books
Website: www.bluebikebooks.com

Library and Archives Canada Cataloguing in Publication

Rowe, Karen, 1975–
    For the love of chocolate / by Karen Rowe.

Includes bibliographical references.

ISBN-13: 978-1-897278-56-7

    1. Chocolate. 2. Cookery (Chocolate). I. Title.
TX767.C5R69 2009   641.3'374   C2008-905783-X

Project Director: Nicholle Carrière
Project Editor: Nicholle Carrière
Production: Vicky Trickett
Cover Image: Courtesy of Jupiterimages
Cover Design: Joy Dirto
Illustrations: Roger Garcia
Photography Credits: Every effort has been made to accurately credit the
sources of photographs. Any errors or omissions should be reported
directly to the publisher for correction in future editions. Photographs
courtesy of Library of Congress (p. 187); Photos.com (p. 67, p. 69, p. 97,
p. 101, p. 113, p. 124); Tony Rath Photography (p.203, p. 207, Images ©
2008 – JC Cuellar of Tony Rath Photography www.tonyrath.com); Ian
Rowe (p. 225, p. 228); Karen Rowe (p. 220)

We acknowledge the support of the Alberta Foundation for the Arts for
our publishing program.

We acknowledge the financial support of the Government of Canada
through the Book Publishing Industry Development Program (BPIDP)
for our publishing activities.

Canadian   Patrimoine
Heritage   canadien

DEDICATION

I would like to dedicate this book to my parents, for whom this Valentine's Day will mark 40 years of marriage. I have no idea what it takes to sustain a marriage for that long, but I suspect that chocolate had something to do with it.

CONTENTS

ACKNOWLEDGMENTS

This book is the result of a lot of blood, sweat and beers. Support comes in countless different ways, and there are many who supported me long before the contract on this book was ever inked and countless others who have had a direct hand in its completion.

Thanks to my sister and "research assistant" Jane. Even though your evaluation of mint hot chocolate almost got you fired ("It looks green, but it tastes brown"), you have been my biggest champion. Your unconditional support and acceptance every step of the way is appreciated more than I could ever begin to express.

To my brother, Ian, for being such a great example—your willingness to try new things and shift your paradigms on a daily basis propels me to do the same.

Thank you to everyone at Blue Bike Books and Sonnet Press—especially Nicholle Carrière and Lisa Wojna—for all your patience, guidance and practical advice.

To my "agent" and Calgary editor, Maclean Kay—your steadfast, even and useful advice in the early stages of my writing was immeasurably valuable to me. I use your "Journalism School in Five Pages or Less" cheat sheet all the time.

Thanks also to Megan Pratt, for hooking me up with this writing gig in the first place.

Cheers to Sharon and Scott Evans for the generous use of the Ghost Town Cottage, without which, this book would never have gotten its start.

To Laurel, who has made my journey down the road less-traveled a lot more fun and considerably less bumpy.

To my dear friends, Craig and Echo, who have long been the mirrors reflecting the truth back at me.

Props to all the friends and family who so earnestly and unselfishly volunteered to be part of my "Chocolate Focus Group." My appreciation to all who donated recipes, pictures, books, ideas and feedback—I couldn't have done it without you. To the friends who completely ignored me while I finished the book—thank you. And to the friends who completely ignored that request and took me out anyway—I needed that, too. Your friendship sustains and nourishes me like no Brad Pitt brownie ever could.

Lastly, I would like to thank the makers of Corona and Blackbird Espresso for their unassuming yet no less valuable contributions to this writer's cause.

P.S. Laura, you rock.

INTRODUCTION

When I was still an infant, my grandmother came to visit and brought with her a pound of milk chocolate drops from England. To hear my mom tell the story, you'd think I'd been subjected to a fate worse than death. "That was the end of you," she'd say.

I was 10 months old and had never tasted chocolate or sugar before in my life. I was a goner. Only allowed one chocolate drop per day, I would spend that time on Granny's lap slobbering up chocolate dribble like there was no tomorrow.

Nothing much has changed since then; I have been a chocolate enthusiast ever since. So it is with much joy that I find myself writing a book about chocolate. I've learned quite a bit through this process, not the least of which is that folk will take just about anything and deep fry it or dip it in chocolate—sometimes both. I've learned that good-quality chocolate is worth the price; I've learned that chocolate is universal—no matter the country or the culture, it connects us all. Sadly, I've also learned that it is becoming a global crisis. Some of you may be shocked to read about chocolate's bloody past and its sometimes unconscionable present.

It is so interesting to me that chocolate has come full circle. In Aztec society, only royalty was allowed to consume chocolate, a tradition that continued in the Spanish and French courts and traversed the ocean to the U.S. It wasn't until after the Industrial Revolution that chocolate became available to the masses. Experts are now predicting that in 20 years, chocolate resources will be so depleted that it will become a commodity only affordable...to the rich.

Lastly, I have learned that the chocolate industry was built on the backs of dreamers and schemers—behind every great company is an even better story. It is no accident that these companies are at the top of their game. Ambitious, entrepreneurial men striving for bigger and better shaped the chocolate industry. Originally about the people behind the names, the chocolate companies of today are a long way from where they started, but the fascinating rivalries and twists and turns have made my research entertaining and compelling. Hopefully, this will also be your experience.

This book is by no means meant to be a comprehensive, exhaustive or even serious examination of the world of chocolate. It was fun unearthing funky, crazy, bizarre and hilarious factoids from around the globe. If I could make use of James Frey's great words, I would parrot his sentiment that "nothing in this book should be considered accurate or reliable." There are vast amounts of information, truth, legend, fact and fiction out there, and I have done my best to present an even, fair and unpredictable account of the world of chocolate. I have tried to capture its cultural significance throughout history and give a glimpse into its future while still keeping everything interesting and fun. The book will hopefully read like a good piece of chocolate—simple, delicious and sinful. And like a Godiva campaign once said: "If chocolate is your downfall, you might as well enjoy the trip."

THE MESO-AMERICANS

Circa 1000 BC

Chocolate in its present-day form is a far cry from the *kakawa* that Olmec women first began using more than 3000 years ago. It was believed that chocolate was made during this time through a rudimentary process of pulverizing the bitter cacao beans into a gummy, gelatinous paste and combining it with water and maize.

Although this combination sounds wretched to our present-day gastronomical sensibilities, it was actually a practical and ingenious recipe. The starchy maize soaked up much of the fatty cocoa butter and made it more digestible, while the rich flavor of the beans made the mixture more palatable. The thick, potent gruel would have been filling, nutritious and energy producing. The Olmec believed it had healing properties and, therefore, made cacao a staple of their diet.

AD 100 to 200

The Olmec mysteriously disappeared around the same time that the Mayan civilization began to dominate. The Izapan were a people closely associated with the Olmec and likely passed on the secrets of chocolate to the Maya.

The Maya lived in what is now Belize, Honduras, Guatemala and the Yucatan Peninsula of Mexico. These lush and fruitful lands were ideal for growing some of the best cacao on the planet. Known today as the Criollo bean, this variety of cacao is still some of the most sought after.

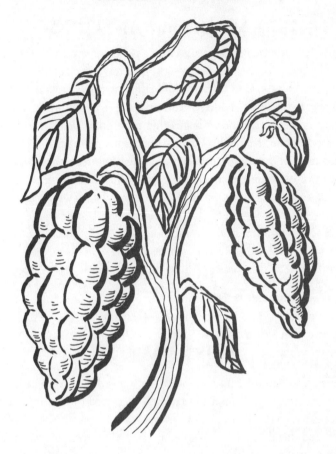

Cocoa Currency

The Mayans used cacao beans as a form of currency. It was so valuable, in fact, that some would try to counterfeit cacao beans by painting pieces of clay or stones to make them resemble cacao beans. Counterfeiters were also known to drill small holes in the beans and fill them with dirt.

You could purchase a rabbit for four cacao beans, the services of a prostitute for 10 beans or a wife or a medium-quality slave for 100 beans. However, a turkey would set you back 200 beans.

Mayan Innovations

The Maya improved the pasty Olmec concoction only slightly by mixing ground cacao beans with a variety of spices, chili peppers, flowers, vanilla, herbs and edible dyes. The plant *achiote*, for example, added a blood red color to the drink. The Maya used only old, worn beans that were no longer fit for currency to make the blend. They were not rich enough to drink their money. Sometimes honey was added to sweeten the brew, but most often, it was mixed with ground corn, making the drink a kind of watery porridge. Called *cacahuatl*, which literally means "cocoa water," the beverage was only ever served to lords, high-ranking warriors and honored dinner guests. Pouring it produced a head of frothy bubbles on the drink—called "scum" by the Europeans—that was consumed first as a "special treat."

DID YOU KNOW?

Cacao also had links to religious rituals and the worship of several Mayan gods. Humans were often sacrificed to guarantee a good cacao harvest, and Aztec priests would wash the blood off their sacrificial knives with hot chocolate and give the drink to those awaiting sacrifice to calm their nerves. Legend has it that the Maya also believed drinking the hot chocolate would convert the victim's heart into a cacao pod, which was then offered to the gods.

THE AZTECS

Montezuma, the Chocolate King

Montecuhzoma Xocoyotzin, better known as Montezuma II, became the ninth emperor of the Aztecs in 1502. Renowned as a merciless, corrupt and decadent tyrant, his greed and gluttony also extended to his consumption of *cacahuatl*. Never known for doing anything half-heartedly, Montezuma was as fervent with his chocolate as he was with his women and his kingdom, and was therefore later known as the "Chocolate King."

Liquid cocoa was served at the end of every meal, though Montezuma drank cups of the frothy, bitter chocolate between courses as well. He never drank from the same cup twice and reportedly threw his golden goblets into the lake beside his palace. In later years, the lake turned out quite literally to be a gold mine for the Spanish.

Cacao was such a valued commodity in the Aztec empire that it served as the official currency of the kingdom. At the height of his empire, Montezuma had a stash of nearly a billion cacao beans.

The Aztecs were also the first to develop solid chocolate bars. Given to Montezuma's warriors as a portable form of nourishment, the tablets were dissolved in water to make a drink. The restorative properties of cocoa could sustain a soldier all day long, and it is believed to have contributed to the force and strength of the indomitable Aztec warriors.

DID YOU KNOW?

In 1502, Christopher Columbus was given cacao pods as a gift upon his arrival on the isle of Guanaja in Honduras. He was one of the first Europeans to try the frothy chocolate beverage and is said to have disliked it.

Cacao or Cocoa?

As a result of a misspelling of the word *cacao*, it became *cocoa* throughout the English-speaking world. Cacao now broadly refers to the tree that grows the pods and at any stage before the beans are processed. Inside the cacao pods are the beans that are the main ingredient for chocolate. Technically they are cacao beans, but they are known throughout the cocoa industry as cocoa beans. Both terms are generally interchangeable.

There is also a theory that the name change occurred when the Spanish conquered Central America. They could not bear the thought of associating cacao with excrement, which they commonly referred to as *kaka*.

1519: The Arrival of the Spanish

Hernan Cortés, a Spanish conqueror, more commonly known as a conquistador, arrived in the Yucatan Peninsula to secure more territory for his emperor, Charles V of Spain. Like Columbus, Cortés never really liked *cacahuatl*, but he did understand its worth.

Finding *cacahuatl* a little bitter, Spanish priests and monks of the time added sugar to the chocolate drink to make it a little more palatable. One of the earliest forms of hot chocolate was concocted by Dominican missionaries, who added cinnamon, black pepper, Cuban sugar, almonds, hazelnuts and *achiote*, a red-colored dye, and then heated the mixture. This modified version of *cacahuatl* appealed to Spanish taste buds and became known as *chocolatl*.

Drinking in Church

Though it is commonly believed that Cortés brought the first cacao beans to Charles V in 1528, it was more likely that priests and monks brought the bitter drink to Europe. The conquistadors saw cocoa only as a monetary treasure and not a gastronomical one.

SUGAR AND SPICE AND EVERYTHING NICE

Had it not found its way as the drink of the Catholic princesses of Spain into the aristocratic society of a sober-minded Europe, [chocolate] would surely have been condemned as a witches' brew.
—Christian Teubner, *The Chocolate Bible*

Chocolate Comes to Europe

Imagine what it would have been like the first time you tasted chocolate in the late 1500s. The average 16th-century diet consisted of bread, porridge, cabbage, carrots and, if you were rich, meat. Your choice of beverages would have included wine, ale or water. Coffee wasn't even introduced to Europe until 1615, and tea much later. Desserts, ice cream and other indulgences didn't exist. Food served the practical purpose of providing the body with nutrients and nothing more. In the 1500s, sugar and spices were only just becoming widely available, but generally, it was unknown to have a food that brought pleasure, delight and extravagance to the palate. Then in comes chocolate, with its rich, filling cocoa butter to awaken the taste buds and excite the senses. It was a taste sensation that swept across the salons of the European elite, beginning in Spain.

Originally served as a cold, thick drink, chocolate eventually evolved into a hot luxury beverage, served in a chocolate pot. These intricate and opulent pots became symbols of Spanish fortune and affluence, and the drink itself represented lavish extravagance and excess—something that has never really changed, even today.

Almost 100 years after it was introduced to Spain, chocolate made its way to Italy via an aristocrat named Antonio Carletti, who introduced the vogue to the Italian upper class in 1606.

DID YOU KNOW?

In the 16th century, before chocolate became so popular, Dutch and British pirates are reputed to have thrown boatloads of cacao overboard in disgust, not recognizing its economic or cultural importance.

1615: Chocolate Arrives at the French Court

We have Anne of Austria to thank for bringing chocolate to France. The king of Spain's daughter, only 15 at the time, married Louis XIII in 1615 and brought with her a penchant for chocolate and a handful of her favorite recipes. The debonair gift of Spanish chocolate was included in the bride's dowry. Neglected by her husband for more than 20 years, it is no surprise that she needed the soothing effects of chocolate. It was only after his death in 1643 that the queen began insisting that others share her passion. She had her lover, the Cardinal of Mazarin, hire a personal chocolatier recruited from Italy.

Chocolate in the Court of Louis XIV

In 1659, Louis XIV granted a monopoly on chocolate to David Chaillou and allowed him to open the first chocolate shop in Paris. He was one of the first chocolatiers, and his shop helped bring chocolate to a growing number of people.

In 1660, cacao was introduced to the island of Martinique by another Spanish princess, Maria Theresa of Austria, who married Louis XIV. Legend has it that she had two passions—the king and…chocolate. She reportedly arrived with a maidservant who knew how to prepare the warm indulgence perfectly.

Louis XIV considered chocolate to be "a food which satisfies hunger but does not fill the stomach" and tried to communicate his aversion to the queen…in vain.

At Versailles, chocolate became all the rage. It was served on Mondays, Wednesdays and Thursdays in the salons of the court.

Madame de Maintenon, secret second wife of Louis XIV, insisted that chocolate be served at the sumptuous feasts held at Marly and Versailles. The king consented for a short period of time, then changed his mind for economic reasons. But it was too late—the queen's passion for chocolate was contagious and spread from the court into the salons of the French aristocracy. As had been the case in the Spanish court, chocolate grew to be a symbol of wealth and prosperity, and it became *à la mode* to offer chocolate to visitors.

The Newest Sensation

From France, word spread to England, then to Denmark, Switzerland and Austria. By the 1650s, the wonders of chocolate were being touted throughout Europe. As it spread, the notoriety of the dark knight increased, until it seemed that it could do just about anything—save children from burning buildings, raise your offspring, do laundry. There was nothing this frothy crusader couldn't do!

In all seriousness, 18th-century society latched onto chocolate with what can best be described as suspicious enthusiasm. Europeans were uncertain whether chocolate was a pleasure or a curse, an indulgence or a drug. The yet-to-be-determined nature of this new product incited many fluctuating opinions concerning chocolate in the 17th and 18th centuries. It was still a mystery to many and was either loved or mistrusted by the elite. Generally, at this time, anything that brought one too much pleasure wasn't to be trusted. It was often considered to be the work of the Devil, and many went about trying to define the role of chocolate in society. It is surprising that chocolate—the "dark drink," as it was called—ever became mainstream at all, given the stranglehold of the Catholic Church on society at the time.

DID YOU KNOW?

Until the 18th century, chocolate was made by monks and nuns, both in Europe and Latin America, using methods handed down from the Aztecs.

Chocolate and the Church

During the ecclesiastical era, it became necessary to define whether chocolate was food or drink, since according to Catholic doctrine, if it was food, followers were not allowed to consume it during Lent. Drinks, however, were permitted, so if chocolate was a drink, then the Lenten fast was not broken. Pope Pius V loathed chocolate and, in 1659, declared it unacceptable to drink. Only three years later, in 1662, Cardinal Brancaccio of Rome decreed that although one couldn't deny that chocolate nourished, it could not be declared a food, and therefore drinking it would not spoil a fast.

Chocolate Ignorance
In 1671, a lady of the French court, Madame de Sévigné, demonstrated the ignorance and passion of the day surrounding chocolate when she held a newborn baby and proclaimed that chocolate was to blame for the color of the child's skin. She believed that the mother—a close friend of hers—had consumed so much chocolate during her pregnancy that it had caused the baby to turn brown.

The superiority of chocolate, both for health and nourishment, will soon give it the same preference over tea and coffee in America which it has in Spain.
—Thomas Jefferson, in a 1785 letter to John Adams

Chocolate Houses, the Latest Fad

Throughout the rest of Europe, just as in Spain and France, serving guests a cup of chocolate became a sign of social prominence and gentility. In 1657, the first chocolate house in England opened to anyone who could afford the entrance fee. During this era, chocolate houses became as popular as coffee houses and taverns. There were chocolate houses that catered only to certain clientele such as poets, politicians or gamblers. The houses became an important part of social life and were bastions of gossip, politics, business and the pursuit of pleasure.

Dickens Disapproves
In *A Tale of Two Cities*, Charles Dickens portrays the drinking of chocolate as a luxury of the idle upper class.

Men Behaving Badly

Many patrons of chocolate houses were handsome, gallant young gentlemen known as "bloods." Some houses were rowdier than others, resulting occasionally in sword fights or brawls. It is possible that the chocolate in some of these establishments was diluted with wine or some form of liquor. In the British society of the day, it was perfectly acceptable for the "right people" to do the "wrong things," so long as they did so with flair and gusto.

By the latter half of the 18th century, most successful chocolate houses in England had become private clubs, generating revenue from affluent members of society rather than the riff-raff that composed the general public. The privatization of coffee houses laid the foundation for the London clubs that would serve as the city's male social hideouts for the next two centuries.

England wasn't the only country to have chocolate houses. In 1697, the visiting mayor of Zurich took his first sip at a chocolate house in Belgium and was mesmerized with the potion, carrying it back to Switzerland with him. Centuries later, both countries would grow to become world leaders in chocolate production.

Really Hot Chocolate
King Friedrich of Prussia sometimes liked to drink his chocolate with pepper and mustard.

Supply and Demand

Throughout the 17th and 18th centuries, chocolate was an important factor in European colonization. Spain initially ruled the cacao trade, with cacao groves in Mexico, Columbia, the Philippines and parts of the Caribbean. But every country that learned about chocolate wanted to secure its own supply. In the 17th century, the Dutch, who were great navigators, took over Spain's cacao monopoly and gained control of the world market.

And Finally, Germany

Germany was one of the last European countries to embrace chocolate and extol its virtues. Still preoccupied as it was with losses incurred from the Thirty Years' War (1618–1648), Germany was focused on rebuilding itself. Consequently, chocolate did not take the main stage in Germany until 1679. Even then, the fashionable drink was so heavily taxed that only the rich were able to enjoy it.

SJOKOLADE
in Afrikaans

INVENTIONS ABOUND

Making Chocolate Available to the Masses

In 1732, a Frenchman name Dubisson invented a table mill for grinding cacao, rendering production easier and chocolate more affordable. From that time onwards, inventions for simplifying the rough confection proliferated.

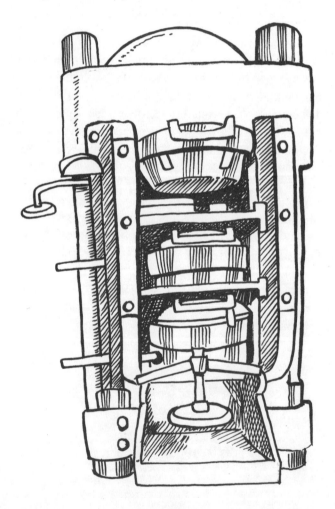

Chocolate Metamorphosis

Chocolate has evolved considerably since the 17th century, when it was like a mafia hitman—strong, bitter and coarse. It was also loaded with so much fat that it would have been difficult to digest. Fillers such as acorn powder, barley and rice were added to try to reduce its intensity, but not surprisingly, did little to improve it. Enter an enterprising Dutch chemist named Coenraad van Houten, who figured out how to separate the fat from the cacao bean.

In 1815, Casparus van Houten set up a small, primitive cocoa mill in his house in Amsterdam. Run by manpower, the pivot of the mill was kept in motion, quite comically no doubt, by laborers running around in circles. In 1828, Casparus patented a hand-operated cocoa press, though his son Coenraad has most commonly been given credit for the invention. Traditionally, chocolate was made straight from roasted cacao beans, which were ground to a smooth paste. With the help of his new invention, Casparus was able to squeeze the heavy paste, filtering out about two-thirds of the cocoa butter. The remaining cakes could be pulverized into a fine powder, known ever since as cocoa. Until this time, the cocoa cakes would spoil easily and become rancid because they still retained all of the cocoa fats.

SAKALADA
in Belarusian

23

Chocolate Production Moves Full-Steam Ahead

Thanks to new technology created during the Industrial Revolution, the chocolate that we know and love today went through some major changes, moving chocolate from its adolescence into adulthood. No longer just a drink for the rich, powdered cocoa lasted longer, becoming mass-produced and widely available. Here's how:

- **Industrial production:** The preparation of cocoa powder became mechanized. Building on van Houten's invention, the hand-operated press was replaced by a steam-powered one, increasing output and efficiency. Cacao beans were placed in steam-driven grinders, where the heat generated by the friction of grinding melted the cocoa butter contained in the beans. Part of the cocoa butter was pressed out under high pressure. The remaining mass was pressed into flat, round cakes and became the raw material for cocoa powder and chocolate.

- **Increased international trade:** Not only did more colonies begin producing cocoa, but improved, more efficient cultivation and planting methods were introduced, which allowed for increased production. The demand of the international cocoa trade required increased cultivation, which resulted in more competitive prices, making cocoa products more affordable.

- **Improved taste:** Adding milk and sugar made the cocoa less bitter and more palatable.

- **Lower taxes:** Until the mid-19th century, chocolate was heavily taxed, much like tobacco is today.

An Army Marches on Its Stomach

The French leader Napoleon insisted that wine from the Burgundy vineyard of Chambertin as well as chocolate be provided during military campaigns. Because of its scarcity and high taxes, mostly caused by Napoleon himself, the distribution of chocolate was limited to himself and his senior military advisors.

One hundred years later, chocolate was still being used to feed soldiers. During the Anglo-Boer War (1899–1902), Queen Victoria sent specially produced chocolates from Great Britain to South Africa as a New Years' gift for her troops.

BARRY CALLEBAUT, NOT A REAL GUY

Charles Barry and Eugenius Callebaut

One in every four bites of chocolate in the world comes from Zurich-based Barry Callebaut, a multi-national chocolate-manufacturing company that proudly claims 25 percent of the market share of the raw chocolate that is processed into candy bars, cocoa and pastries. But if you are looking to meet the famous chocolatier behind the name, you might be disappointed to learn that there isn't one.

The name actually belongs to two men, both of whom began with modest but ambitious roots.

A Frenchman named Charles Barry opened a tea and coffee business in 1842. His passion for chocolate eventually led him to Africa to seek out a selection of cacao beans that would make it possible for him to create a thriving business. Callebaut was founded by Eugenius Callebaut as a brewery in Wieze, Belgium, in 1850, and began producing chocolate bars in 1911.

Barry Callebaut was created in the 1996 merger of the Belgian company Callebaut with rival French company Cacao Barry and today operates in 25 countries worldwide.

It Runs in the Family

For Canadians familiar with Calgary-based chocolatier Bernard Callebaut, it may come as no surprise that Bernard is one of Eugenius Callebaut's great-great-grandsons. Though related, Bernard and his chocolaterie are not affiliated with the Barry Callebaut company.

NOT JUST FOR THE RICH ANYMORE

The Quakers

One interesting fact about chocolate in England was that the Quakers participated very heavily in this business.

Quakers were religious pacifists who rebuffed the Church of England, believing that they didn't need any institutions to mediate their relationship with God. Refusing to pledge an oath to the British Crown, Quakers were barred from attending universities or owning land. In the 17th century, thousands of

Quakers were imprisoned or banished, many of them fleeing to the colonies. For example, William Penn, founder of Pennsylvania, was a Quaker.

By the 19th century, the Church of England had loosened its grip on religious divergence, and Quakers began to assimilate more easily. Quakers were industrious and successful entrepreneurs and became prominent leaders in the production of cocoa. The Quakers hoped to persuade the poor to give up drinking alcohol in favor of the healthier chocolate drink.

DID YOU  KNOW?

Cadbury, Fry and Rowntree were all founded by Quakers.

The Fry Family: Industrial Revolutionists

Joseph Fry, a Quaker doctor, took over a chocolate-making company in 1769 after the death of its founders. His grandson figured out how to mass-produce cocoa by combining van Houten's cocoa press with a steam-powered hydraulic press, revolutionizing the industry. The Frys were also the first to introduce a rudimentary chocolate bar in 1847. The company blended small amounts of melted, clarified cocoa butter with sugar, flavor and cocoa solids and molded it into a bar that melted on your tongue. Affordable, mass-produced and sweet, the bar helped J.S. Fry & Sons become the world's leading chocolate producers.

But the Frys had competition from other Quakers—the Cadbury brothers.

The Cadburys: Marketing Masterminds

One of 10 children, John Cadbury opened up a grocery store in Birmingham in 1824, where he ground his own cacao beans

using a mortar and pestle. He probably never suspected that from these humble beginnings, his company would become one of the largest conglomerate empires in the world.

In 1847, Benjamin Cadbury joined his brother as a partner in the company. John Cadbury retired in 1861, handing over the business to his eldest sons, Richard and George. The Cadburys had something that set them apart from the other companies— they were excellent marketers, something that even today has not really changed. The Cadburys used cute and clever packaging, which appealed to the sentiments of Victorian customers. They were the first to attach chocolate to feelings, and we have the Cadbury brothers to thank for being the first to come up with the marketing behemoth that is Valentine's Day. It was also the Cadbury brothers who sold the first chocolate Easter egg as a reward to mark the end of the sacrificial Lenten period, linking their product to one of the most important celebrations on the Christian calendar.

Until the 1800s, people bought their chocolate in apothecary shops because it was considered a wholesome food that had medicinal value. It was sold along with other stimulants such as tobacco. The Cadbury brothers were the ones who changed chocolate from a medicinal necessity into an indulgent pleasure that gratified the senses, elevating its status from serf to goddess.

The Rowntrees: Leaders in Employee Treatment

The son of a Quaker grocer, Joseph Rowntree dedicated most of his life working to improve the lives of his staff. He led the way in the humane and ethical treatment of his workforce, which was unheard of at the time in England. Rowntree provided a library in the factory, education for employees under the age of 17, free medical and dental services and a pension fund. He also paved the way for modern-day corporations. His factory was a far cry from the sweatshops that ruled England at the time.

The Quakers also laid the groundwork for a new era in which wealth was no longer determined by bloodline. The Rowntrees believed that hard work and clean living paved the path to success.

But capitalism also caused enormous social problems, as greed and money planted their seeds. Seebohm Rowntree, Joseph's son, was considered a "moral businessman," an oxymoron in today's lexicon. He worked towards the establishment of Britain's first welfare system, which included a minimum wage for employees and a family allowance. Rowntree employees were treated to a clean, safe and democratic working environment— they worked in shifts, were fairly paid, received their salaries and benefits on a regular and scheduled basis and could even choose their own managers. The rights and responsibilities of workers and their managers were posted in writing.

Seebohm Rowntree believed his company was there to be of service to others and not to generate revenue.

The Rowntrees weren't the only "gentle giants." The Cadburys, appalled by the working conditions of 19th-century British factories, moved their operation to the countryside. In 1878, the company purchased 14 1/2 acres of land on the banks of the Bourn River near Birmingham and began to build their community. With green spaces for relaxation and a dining room for wholesome meals, Bournville was meant to inspire employees and create healthy surroundings. To this day, Bournville is a tourist attraction.

Being Quakers, the Cadbury brothers promoted church attendance and a principled way of life among their employees. Bibles were given as wedding gifts, and newly married women were expected to leave the factory and become housewives. Pubs and drinking establishments were banned in Bournville. This moral righteousness would plague the company years later amid allegations of sustaining the slave trade.

The unlikely and nurturing Quakers became industry leaders in cocoa. But capitalism would rear its bitter, ugly head. Ironically, the Quaker companies that were known for the principled treatment of their employees turned a blind eye when it came to the origins of their raw material. Out of sight, out of mind. Having set the bar so high, these clean-living, church-attending teetotalers would be held to a higher corporate and moral standard and become easy targets for critics in the years that followed.

Does Willy Wonka Really Exist?
No, although Roald Dahl did base *Willy Wonka and the Chocolate Factory* on historical fact. Specifically, the book references the intense competition between Cadbury and Rowntree, who constantly accused one another of industrial espionage.

The Big Three

The Big Three (Mars, Nestlé and Hershey in North America) are still intensely paranoid. In the UK, the Big Three are Mars, Nestlé and Cadbury, and they control 74 percent of the market. The dominance of the Big Three can be explained by the high costs of production and marketing involved in launching a new product. It is estimated that the cost of launching a new chocolate product in mainland Britain is £100 million, or about $2.2 million USD.

Fry's was eventually taken over by Cadbury in 1916. In 1969, Cadbury merged with Schweppes to become one of the largest international companies in the world. Cadbury still tries to integrate its socially progressive roots with its business.

 ### The Cadbury Creme Egg
Today Cadbury is better known more for its Creme Egg than its social politics. The first Cadbury Creme Egg was introduced in 1923. Available only between New Years' and Easter, the modern Cadbury egg we all know and love wasn't created until 1971.

The Creme Egg plant in Bournville can produce 70,000 eggs an hour, 50 million chocolate pieces a day, 598 chocolate bars a minute and 1800 tons of chocolate a week.

SIKWATE
in Boholano

OTHER GREAT CONFECTIONERS GET THEIR START

1819
François-Louis Cailler opens one of the first mechanized chocolate factories, from which the firm known as Nestlé is born.

1826
In Serriers, Switzerland, Philippe Suchard opens a chocolate factory based on the first chocolate shop that opened the year before in Neuchâtel.

1879
In Bern, Switzerland, Rudolphe Lindt perfects the recipe for dark chocolate through a technique called conching. In this process, liquid chocolate is swept back and forth with large paddles for several hours to produce the smoothest chocolate ever, which Lindt names chocolate fondant. It is the first reliable melting chocolate, making it perhaps one of the most significant advances in chocolate making to date. In 1899, Rudolph Lindt sells his recipes and conching technology to David Sprüngli, marking the beginning of Swiss industry giant Lindt & Sprüngli.

1908
Jean Tobler of Switzerland introduces his Toblerone bar.

1913
Swiss confectioner Jules Sechaud invents bonbons, the first chocolates with unique fillings.

1926
Belgian chocolatier Joseph Draps begins a small praline-making business in his home in Brussels. Wishing to expand, he opens a chocolate store and, upon his wife's suggestion, decides to adopt

Lady Godiva, who represents luxury and decadence, as its logo. In 1966, Godiva is bought out by soup giant, Campbell's. Today, it is one of the best-known chocolate companies in America, and the plant in Reading, Pennsylvania, now produces as much chocolate for the American market as the Belgian plant produces for the rest of the world.

A Room Full of Chocolate

Can't get enough chocolate? Neither can the chocolatiers at Godiva, who create an extravagant chocolate promotion for their customers every year. In 2008, a Decadence Suite was crafted— an all-chocolate room complete with chocolate furniture and artwork. The lucky contestant who bought the winning box of chocolates was treated to the ultimate chocolate fantasy—a pampered getaway weekend for two in the suite. Not only did the winners get to stay on a bed decorated with chocolates while reading books from the chocolate bookcases and staring at the chocolate walls, chandeliers and coffee table, but the package also included a Godiva chocolate tasting. Other perks included a chocolate spa experience, a private gourmet meal and wine pairing, and as if that wasn't enough, the lucky romantics were also supplied with a year's worth of Godiva chocolate. The previous year's contest awarded chocoholics with a $1 million diamond shopping spree.

1970

Tobler and Suchard become one of the largest chocolate groups in Europe when the two companies merge.

SHOKOLAD
in Bulgarian

THE ITALIANS: MASTERS OF HAZELNUT

Turin, Italy's Chocolate Heart

Today Turin and the surrounding area are leaders in Italy for chocolate production, with an output of 85,000 tons, or 40 percent of the country's chocolate production. Italy has had a rich and unique affair with chocolate, and there have been many pioneers in Turin's chocolate industry.

The Savoy Family

The history of chocolate in Turin and in Piedmont would probably look and taste different had it not been for the Savoy family.

In 1559, Emanuele Filiberto of Savoy returned to Spain bearing cacao seeds. The following year, to celebrate the transfer of the Italian capital from Chambery to Turin, he symbolically served a steaming cup of hot chocolate to the city.

In 1587, Caterina, daughter of Philip II of Spain, married Carlo Emanuele I, son of Emanuele Filiberto. For the wedding, the cooks of the royal palace made much ado about preparing and serving hot chocolate to the guests.

Madame Reale, ruler of the Savoy throne, granted the first "license" to Turinese chocolate maker Giò Antonio Ari in 1678. The license allowed him to process, produce and sell chocolate. Until that time, makers of chocolate-based beverages were not allowed to sell it. Known as *limonadiers* in Turin, they were confectioners and liquor vendors, though many of them came from court circles. Only café owners could serve chocolate along with coffee and other hot and cold beverages. Madame Reale's decree changed all that, and the *cicôlatè 'd Turin*, or professional chocolate chef, became a high-profile figure.

During the 1700s, thanks to the Savoys and their connections with the Madrid court, Turin became the chocolate capital of the world.

The First Chocolate Bars

During the early 19th century, Paolo Caffarel opened a chocolate production facility on the banks of the Pellerina canal in Turin. Caffarel used a water wheel to supply energy for the machinery inside his factory. A mixer designed by Bozelli from Genoa allowed the production of about 770 pounds of chocolate per day.

This was the birth of the chocolate industry—the culmination of the process that had begun in the 1700s. During the 18th century, Turinese chocolate makers began to use simple machines that allowed the chocolate to solidify, thus allowing for the production of bars, whereas chocolate had previously only been consumed as a beverage.

The *Gianduiotto*

The *gianduiotto* is Turin's most famous and well-known chocolate confection. Originally carried out manually, the process involved blending cocoa and roasted hazelnuts into a paste until it had a smooth and consistent texture. The chocolate maker then ladled out the chocolate, giving it the shape of an upturned boat, which is now one of its best-known characteristics.

With mechanization, *gianduiotti* were later formed by extrusion, meaning that the chocolate-hazelnut paste was forced through a specially shaped mold or nozzle, producing a continuous strip that was then cut by hand.

Although the extrusion technique is faster, handmade *gianduiotti* are often preferred to the mechanized versions because they are less elastic, less fatty and have a longer-lasting hazelnut flavor.

All Wrapped Up
The *gianduiotto* was the first chocolate in the world to ever be wrapped in paper.

Did Napoleon Play a "Bonaparte" in the Development of the Classic Italian Chocolate?

Could Napoleon Bonaparte be called the father of the *gianduiotto*? Well, technically, no, but it does make for a great story.

In 1806, Napoleon was adamant about preventing his enemies, namely the British, from trading with continental Europe. Signing the Berlin Decree, he imposed a blockade, meaning that all trading and shipments to and from England were stopped. This of course affected all of Europe, and since the blockade lasted for most of the 19th century, it turned cocoa into a rare commodity and made it difficult to continue producing chocolate.

Raw cocoa was so expensive that local producers began incorporating bits of locally grown, inexpensive hazelnuts into chocolate to make the final product more affordable. In 1852, Michele Prochet, an enterprising young chocolate maker, was the first to completely grind roasted hazelnuts to a paste before adding them to the cocoa and sugar mixture. The result of this mixture was the *gianduia* paste, used to make the *gianduiotto*. In the beginning, this special chocolate with its irregular boat shape was called *givu*, which in Piedmontese means "cigarette butt." It wasn't until 1865 that this specialty became known as *gianduia*, the name given to the Carnival mask of Turin.

The Gianduiotto Code

A parody of the bestseller *The Da Vinci Code*, *Il codice Gianduiotto*, or *The Gianduiotto Code*, is a novel that centers on the mysteries of the secret formula for the *gianduiotto*.

Liquid Ecstasy: *Bicerin di Gianduiotto*

Those fortunate enough to have sampled this Italian chocolate liqueur say it's better than being in love. Touted as an alcoholic version of a liquid Ferrero Rocher, the intoxicating aroma has helped to make this the preferred drink of the Turinese for the past 200 years. Great on ice cream, as a cocktail, a dessert or a cake ingredient or with *panettonne* (a sweet Italian bread), this liquid ecstasy is very versatile and can also be served in coffee or as a digestif when mixed with rum, whisky or vodka.

Il Bacio Perugina

In 1922, in her shop in Perugia, Luisa Spagnoli mixed hazelnut grains with chocolate to create a new chocolate called *cazzotto*, or "punch," because of its fist-like shape. But it was Giovanni Buitono, one of the founders of the Perugina chocolate company, who changed the name to *bacio*, or "kiss."

Ferrero: Italian Chocolatier Extraordinaire

In 1946, the Ferrero company was still relatively new by Italian standards. After the war, candy and confections were in short supply and were purchased mainly for special occasions from local confectioners. Pietro Ferrero, a master confectioner in the small town of Alba, developed a system that enabled him to mass-produce true quality confections and offer them to consumers at reasonable prices. Ferrero went on to introduce many of the best-known confections in the world.

The first Ferrero product was *Pasta Gianduja*, a chocolate-hazelnut spread that became the number-one-selling sweet spread in the world. The product was renamed, and on April 20, 1964, the first jar of Nutella was produced.

Ferrero also gets credit for creating a liqueur-filled praline with a cherry inside called Mon Chéry in 1956.

In 1968, Ferrero launched the Kinder trademark, which sells Kinder Surprise and Kinder Bueno.

But it was in 1982 that Ferrero produced what would become the best-selling chocolate in the world. A whole, roasted hazelnut was encased in a thin wafer shell filled with hazelnut cream, then covered in milk chocolate and chopped hazelnuts—the praline-filled hazelnut and chocolate shell, named the Ferrero Rocher, was a force to be reckoned with. Ferrero Rocher remains a popular gift during the holidays, especially during Chinese New Year. Chinese culture associates the gold of the packaging with good fortune and wealth.

COCOA AND THE SLAVE TRADE

Slaving to Meet Growing Demand

By the 1800s, the Spanish had completely depleted the cocoa plantations in Central America. Other countries discovered that cacao beans could be grown within 20 degrees of the equator and began exploiting Third World countries in Africa and Asia to meet the growing demand for chocolate. Africans had been working as slaves for years—a practice, unfortunately, that wouldn't immediately change. Reports of dreadful slave-labor practices began to appear as early as the 1850s from the Portuguese African cocoa islands of São Tomé and Principe and intensified in both number and severity until well into the 1890s and beyond.

The Islands of No Return
Records show that none of the workers sent to the islands of São Tomé and Principe ever returned.

Turning a Blind Eye

Cadbury Bros. Ltd. was a Quaker-owned chocolate manufacturer in England known for its social ethics and high-quality chocolates, which at the time purchased almost half of its cocoa from São Tomé and Principe. Cadbury Bros. likely knew about the appalling conditions in the Portuguese islands, but had no idea what to do about them.

In 1901, chocolate heir William Cadbury visited Lisbon to investigate the allegations of slavery, but Portuguese authorities assured him that his suspicions were unfounded and that reports of slavery were "highly exaggerated." They invited Cadbury to see for himself, which he eventually did, but not until many years later.

Slavery Under a Different Name

First, Cadbury decided to open their own investigation, but dragged their feet considerably in organizing its launch. Somewhat reluctantly, they did eventually send an English Quaker by the name of Joseph Burtt to the cocoa plantations in 1905. Burtt observed that nearly half of the newly arrived laborers at one of the plantations had been forcibly recruited and died within a year. He concluded that the workers, though called "contract laborers," were never paid and, for all intents and purposes, were still treated as slaves.

Making Changes

William Cadbury himself visited both Principe and São Tomé, but not until 1908, when public outcry could no longer be ignored. On his way there, Cadbury made a pit stop on the Gold Coast, now called Ghana, and secured himself an alternate supply of cocoa. Once that resource of cocoa was in place, and not before, the company proceeded with its boycott of the Portuguese West African islands.

Slave Trade Boycott

Twenty years after the time that initial reports surfaced about slave-labor practices and a full seven years from the time that Cadbury first reported these issues to its board of directors, the company finally took action. In November 1909, Cadbury announced that it would no longer buy Portuguese cacao and persuaded two other cocoa manufacturers, Fry and Rowntree, to join them. In 1910, Stollwerck Bros. of Cologne joined the boycott. Even so, conditions improved only marginally, and slavery continued on the islands for many more years. Africans working in São Tomé and Principe were still forced into labor until the 1950s.

Ongoing Grief

Despite the United States' Slave Emancipation Proclamation issued by Abraham Lincoln in 1863, American companies resisted the boycott of Portuguese cacao.

Regardless of worldwide condemnation of slavery and laws against it, as many as eight million Africans died from overwork or were slaughtered by their masters in the late 19th and early 20th centuries.

Xocolata
in Catalan

MODERN-DAY MISERY

Slavery Today

Unfortunately, slavery isn't relevant only to the past. Today, there are an estimated 12 million people still in slavery around the world. That includes 12,000 child slave laborers trafficked across the borders of the Ivory Coast to work on farms growing cacao beans for use by the world's big chocolate manufacturers.

There are myriad other problems as these African countries struggle to keep up with the growing demand for cacao. Increased market value, underpaid workers, smuggling and corruption are all a blight on the African cocoa trade.

Prices Soar
In the summer of 2008, the price of cocoa soared to an astounding $3150 per tonne, the highest in 28 years, marking a 53 percent increase since 2007. Comparatively, gasoline increased a mere 40 percent in that same time period. Poor African harvests, among other things, have left chocolate stock-piles at a 22-year low.

Smuggled Cacao Beans Impact Supplies from Ghana

Today, Ghana is second only to the Ivory Coast as the largest producer of cacao beans, and corrupt practices still exist. Cacao bean supplies are being compromised by smugglers, which is responsible, in part, for worldwide price increases.

Cacao growers in the Ivory Coast are paid market value for their beans, while in neighboring Ghana, prices are fixed at the beginning of the season. The increased prices encourage smugglers from Ghana to cross the border and sell their product for a higher value. Smuggling is a common problem in all of western Africa, and with cacao bean prices soaring, the appeal of illegal activity is even stronger. The government of Ghana has increased the producer price for cacao by 25 percent in an attempt to stop the flow of smuggled beans to the Ivory Coast and Togo.

John Mason, of the Nature Conservation Research Council based in Ghana, says that "in 20 years, chocolate will be like caviar." This terrible fate is possible mostly because of poor farming practices in Western Africa. Pushed by the high demand, farmers clear-cut sections of rainforest and work the land to death. The problem with that method of farming is that it is not sustainable—cacao trees on the clear-cut land live about 30 years, compared to 75 to 100 years in the rainforest.

Widespread Corruption

Meanwhile, the Ivory Coast has its own share of problems dealing with pervasive corruption in its cocoa industry. The Ivory Coast liberalized its cocoa sector in 2000, ending a system of state-guaranteed prices and setting up a network of agencies meant to promote and regulate the industry. It is the leadership of many of these organizations that has been accused of corruption, and farmers have long called for those administering funds raised from taxes to be replaced.

Over the next three years, some $800 million of funding could be available to the world's top cocoa producer, but the World Bank has said it will not lend money to the country unless it cleans up its act.

In June 2008, numerous senior cocoa officials were arrested after accusations were made alleging that more than $218 million had been stolen. To make matters worse, the country's Coffee and Cocoa Bourse (CCB) was also paralyzed by a strike in the summer of 2008 over the lack of pay and a leadership struggle following the arrest of the previous administration.

Cacao farmers report that the regulatory structures are useless because money is taken from them, but nothing ever changes. Planters are not being paid a fair price for their yield, and some still don't have enough money to buy medicine and basic necessities of life.

It is evident that revenues are being mismanaged, and the Ivory Coast's government has promised reforms, but so far no action has been taken. The Ivory Coast is struggling to organize presidential elections, which are meant to end a crisis sparked by a brief war in 2002 and 2003 and reunite a country that has been divided since rebels seized much of the north.

It is unfortunate that the struggling country is unable to benefit and advance its socio-economic status despite a thriving cocoa industry, high demand and soaring market prices.

Get Ready to Shell Out

So, what does all this mean to the consumer? Barry Callebaut, the company that makes chocolate for groups such as Nestlé and Cadbury, indicated recently that the price of chocolate products will need to rise by up to 18 percent to offset the market price increase of raw materials. Packaging, energy and transport costs have also risen, which means it is going to cost the average consumer more to indulge that sweet tooth.

Slavery-Free Chocolate Sources

If this information has prompted more questions, take the time to research chocolate products and make an informed and thoughtful decision before buying. There are many non-partisan sites on the Internet with information listing chocolate companies that state their cocoa has not been produced with slave labor.

CHOCOLATE CROSSES THE POND

Caramels are only a fad. Chocolate is a permanent thing.
—Milton S. Hershey

Baker, Baker, Bake Me a Cake

One of America's first chocolate makers was actually Irish. John Hannon imported cacao beans from the West Indies into Dorchester, Massachusetts, in 1765. American Dr. James Baker helped Hannon refine the beans and began producing chocolate cakes in America's first chocolate mill. The unsweetened cakes became Baker's chocolate, which is how the term "baking chocolate" came into being.

Fourteen years later, John Hannon disappeared at sea while on a bean-buying voyage, making Baker sole proprietor of their successful chocolate business, which was bought by General Foods in 1927.

In 1872, the Baker Chocolate Company adopted Jean-Étienne Liotard's painting *La Belle Chocolatière* as its trademark, one of the oldest trademarks in the United States.

DID YOU KNOW?

The submarine, the electric streetcar, the camera and the machine gun were all invented before milk chocolate. Milk chocolate was created in Switzerland by Daniel Peter in 1875 after more than eight years of experimentation. Milk chocolate is actually a very tricky thing to make. It took centuries before the art of milk chocolate was mastered. Peter sold his creation to his neighbor, Henri Nestlé, and thus Nestlé chocolate came into being.

THE HERSHEY EMPIRE

Quakers in Colonial America

The Quakers' involvement in chocolate continued with their emigration to colonial America in 1677, primarily to Pennsylvania. It was one of the descendants of those colonial Quakers, Milton Snavely Hershey, who would later become perhaps the most important name in the chocolate industry.

As with the Olmec, the Mayans, the Aztecs and the Europeans, chocolate was a luxury in the U.S. and affordable only by the rich. It was Milton S. Hershey who made chocolate available to the public at large when he began mass-producing his milk chocolate bar.

Hershey failed at his first attempt as a candy maker. He later found success making caramels when he began adding real milk instead of paraffin, which was what most manufacturers were using at the time. But it was in 1893 that Hershey found his life's calling. While visiting the Chicago World's Fair, he stumbled across a chocolate-making machinery exhibit from Germany and was immediately enthralled. Hershey returned to that exhibit each day of the fair to learn more about making chocolate and bought the equipment on the spot. When the fair closed, he moved the chocolate-making machinery to his caramel factory, where he began manufacturing chocolate in a back corner on the third floor of his factory.

Pricing Policy

In 1903, Hershey chocolate bars began selling for five cents each, and there was no price increase until November 24, 1969. Hershey maintained this price by changing the weight of the chocolate bar, which varied from 1.25 ounces to an all-time low of 0.6875 ounces. Eventually, Hershey Inc. had no choice but to increase its price to 10 cents a bar, which caused an outrage among its customers. Hershey stock fell 30 percent in the nine months following the price increase.

DID YOU KNOW?

In the first year, sales from Hershey chocolate bars generated revenue totaling $622,000. Considering that the average salary at this time in the United States for a 60-hour workweek was $12.98 per week, this is a staggering amount. In today's dollars, that would translate to revenue of approximately $14,306,000. In 2007, the Hershey Company generated $4.95 billion revenue for all of its products.

Milking It

Hershey never advertised his chocolate products—business grew by word of mouth, prompting him to move his factory to the country, where he would have access to the fresh milk used in his chocolates. Hershey chose a remote location close to Derry Church, Pennsylvania, where he was born.

Wanting to focus exclusively on chocolate, Hershey sold the Lancaster Caramel Company in 1900 for $1 million, which today would translate to about $24 million.

ČOKOLADA
in Croatian

Hershey Builds His Own Chocolate Mecca

Milton Hershey was an idealist and a dreamer. Just as the Cadbury brothers in England had done, Hershey had a vision of building an entire community for his workforce—a town with employee housing, indoor plumbing and electricity, stores, amenities and a trolley system for employees to commute from surrounding areas. He even built a golf course, a zoo and a 32-acre public garden. In those early days, Hershey served as constable, fire chief and mayor. In 1906, a contest was held for his employees to name the town. They decided on Hersheykoko, but the name was shortened at the request of the U.S. Post Office. This is how the town of Hershey, Pennsylvania, was born.

"Sour" Chocolate

Milton Hershey had to find a way to produce large amounts of affordable, quality, long-lasting milk chocolate. It took him years to perfect his formula, and since Hershey was not a chemist, he kept encountering problems. Milk had to be condensed, and trying to condense cream, which he thought would yield richer chocolate, caused it to burn. The chocolate wouldn't harden, would spoil within a few weeks or would be lumpy.

Finally, by adding a large amount of sugar to the milk, Hershey was able to boil the mixture slowly at a low heat. The resulting chocolate was light brown in color and mild to the taste. In making the solution, Hershey unknowingly hit upon a method that allowed enzymes to break down the remaining milk fat and produce flavorful fatty acids. In other words, Hershey milk chocolate was slightly soured.

Though extremely popular in America, Hershey's unique, fermented chocolate never sold in Europe. A myriad of unsavory adjectives were used by discerning Europeans to describe Hershey chocolate, including "offensive," "inedible," "cheesy" and "raunchy." Most European chocolate merchants believed that Hershey had no idea what he was doing and thought his "discovery" was actually a mistake. They accused Hershey of intentionally using spoiled milk to make his "special chocolate" because he was too cheap to throw it out. These claims, of course, were disputed by Hershey Inc.

Depression-Era Success

It was a great source of pride for Hershey that not one single employee lost his job during the Depression. Hershey found a way to keep his men working by funding various construction projects for the town. Hershey sponsored a theater, gymnasium, swimming pool, library, resort hotel, ice hockey arena, football stadium and one of the first air-conditioned office buildings in America.

Sweet Source

Sugar was scarce during World War II, so Hershey bought sugarcane fields in Cuba and started to refine his own sugar. He built a whole town in Cuba and named it Central Hershey.

DID YOU  KNOW?

The Hershey factory was considered the most modern chocolate- manufacturing facility of its time. Because chocolate was so expensive to make, it was cheaper and more practical to buy it elsewhere, and surprisingly, Mars used to be one of Hershey's best customers. Hershey estimates that the plant provided more than 75 percent of the nation's eating chocolate in the 1940s.

Marketing Genius

Legend has it that whenever Milton Hershey saw one of his company's nickel-bar wrappers on the ground, instead of throwing it away, he turned it face up—his way of advertising.

Lasting Love

In 1909, Hershey opened a school for orphan boys right next to his plant, where the boys received an education and learned a trade. Shortly after the death of his wife in 1915, Hershey discreetly donated his shares of Hershey stock to the school in her memory. He was a very private man, so his generosity was not discovered for another five years. The transfer of his stock was valued at $60 million. Hershey profits continue to support his orphanage even today. Milton Hershey sent flowers to his wife's grave twice a week for the rest of his life.

DID YOU KNOW?

Adventurer Admiral Richard Byrd carried Hershey bars with him during his expeditions to the Antarctic in 1928 and 1932.

The Mayan Warriors Were Onto Something

Just like Montezuma's warriors, soldiers in World War II were provided with high-energy chocolate rations to carry in their pockets. Hershey Foods Corporation helped the U.S. government develop Field Ration D, which was made from a thick paste of chocolate liquor, sugar, oat flour, powdered milk and vitamins. A single serving provided 600 calories and would not melt. It tasted nothing like a regular Hershey bar and had a putty-like texture. Think Silly Putty, only brown and "edible."

While the men were off fighting the war, the women kept the Hershey plant running. In 1942, the factory was open seven days a week and produced 500,000 Ration D bars a day. The company received an award from the government for its contribution to the war effort.

A War Among Suppliers

Later, during Desert Storm and the Gulf War in the early 1990s, Hershey improved the heat-resistant chocolate to withstand the hot sun. The chocolate bar, named the "Desert Bar," was given the catchy slogan: "Melts in your mouth, not in the sand." This obvious dig at Mars was part of a publicity stunt by Hershey Foods Corp to win over the hearts of the American public. Solid at temperatures up to 140°F, almost one million Desert Bars were shipped to the troops free of charge, making the evening news all across the country. Meanwhile, Mars had quietly been distributing slightly altered versions of M&Ms and Galaxy block chocolate to the troops, and it was actually Mars that had won the candy bid. Mars was the government's official candy supplier, not Hershey. This caused anger and bitterness between the companies. Hershey Foods appealed the government's decision, accusing Mars of using too much lactose in the bars and producing a product that was not up to code. Mars was bitter because Hershey was getting all the credit for supporting the troops, and Hershey was angry because they had lost the government contract. It was not the dream that Milton Hershey and Frank Mars had envisioned when they built their companies and collaborated to bring affordable chocolate to the masses.

MARS AND M&Ms

A Worldwide Phenomenon

The most popular chocolate and biggest worldwide seller are M&Ms from Mars Inc. There are 400 million M&Ms made daily and 12 million made hourly.

When Forrest Mars first introduced M&Ms in 1940, his aim was to create a chocolate candy that wouldn't melt. While traveling through Spain during the civil war, Forrest saw soldiers eating chocolate lentils coated with sugary candy. He realized that the chocolate withstood the heat because it was protected by the candy shell. The rest is history.

During World War II, the U.S. Air Force was the largest buyer of M&Ms, which it purchased for its bomber pilots stationed in North Africa and the Pacific theater. The army came in second, distributing the chocolates to soldiers as C-rations.

Few people realize that M&M stands for Murrie and Mars. M&Ms were developed in a cooperative venture between Mars and its now archrival, Hershey. R. Bruce Murrie was the son of William Murrie, Hershey's longtime president and Milton Hershey's dearest friend. Although it is very uncommon now, at the time, it was standard practice for companies to collaborate with competitors.

DID YOU KNOW?

Mars changes the mix of M&M colors to keep in line with consumer tastes. The current mix is 30 percent brown, 20 percent red and yellow and 10 percent orange, blue and green.

From a Different Planet?

Mars is a family-owned business, and the Mars family is one of the wealthiest in the world, with each member worth $10.5 billion.

Mars Inc. is obsessive and secretive about the day-to-day workings of its operations. If Mars requires outside service workers to fix a specific machine, the contractors are blindfolded and accompanied through the plant to the area in question. Once the problem is resolved, the contractors are blindfolded again and courteously escorted from the premises.

Cleanliness First
At the M&M factory in Hackettstown, New Jersey, associates scrub the floor every 45 minutes.

DID YOU  **KNOW?**

Curiously, many chocolate companies also produce high-quality pet food. Mars manufactures all types of food, including Uncle Ben's, Whiskas, Sheba, Kal Kan and Pedigree. Nestlé manufactures Ralston Purina and Friskies. Let's hope they never get them mixed up with the chocolate products. Who would want a candy-coated dog treat?

If at First You Don't Succeed...

Frank Mars failed three times before getting it right. Finally, in 1914, with his last remaining $400, he made one last-ditch effort to start up a successful candy-manufacturing company. However, because of his three previous failed companies, Frank Mars' horrible credit history followed him wherever he went. Consequently, he was unable to buy ingredients in bulk and had to stick to a strict cash-only payment system with the few small candy makers who had agreed to sell him surplus sugar, corn syrup and extracts. Possibly inspired by the company's founder, Mars has to this day stuck with a no-debt policy. Named after a delicious, gooey chocolate bar with caramel and nuts that Frank had invented, the Mar-O-Bar Company was born.

The Milky Way Saves the Mars Universe

The Milky Way gets the credit for saving the Mar-O-Bar Company from financial ruin. Originally a chocolate malted milk drink, Frank Mars added some caramel to the Milky Way and turned it into a chocolate bar. It sold all across the country with no advertising. The Milky Way was a popular bar because it was bigger than other chocolate bars and tasted just as rich as the drink. It cost much less to produce because it was not solid chocolate like the Hershey bar.

The Milky Way filling, a whipped filling made of egg whites and corn syrup, must age for at least two weeks to allow its weightless, fluffy consistency to develop. When it is first made, the nougat center of the candy bar is dense and taffy-like.

A Mars by Any Other Name
The chocolate bar that Americans know and love as the Milky Way is known everywhere else in the world as the Mars Bar. There once was an American Mars, but it was renamed Snickers Almond. Of course, the Milky Way bar does exist outside the U.S., but it tastes much like the American 3 Musketeers bar.

Humble Beginnings

Frank Mars' son, Forrest, was only six years old when his parents divorced. He was sent to live with his grandparents in North Battleford, Saskatchewan, and Forrest didn't see his father again until he was 19.

Forrest spent the rest of his childhood in Canada and graduated from Lethbridge High School in Lethbridge, Alberta, in 1922. He won a partial scholarship to Berkley with plans to become a mining engineer and return to Canada, but candy and chocolate were in his blood and he never returned.

Like Father, Like Son

Forrest Mars did not see his father again until 1923, when Frank came to bail him out of a Chicago jail, after some marketing shenanigans as a traveling salesman had landed him in the slammer. Having grown up believing his father was a terrible failure, Forrest was surprised to learn of his father's success with the Mar-O-Bar Company. Although they hadn't seen one another for more than 13 years, the meeting would prove to be life changing for both of them. Never having been close, the two realized that they had one thing in common—a passion for business.

All for One...
Created in 1932, Mars' 3 Musketeers bar was named after its original recipe, which layered three pieces of nougat candy—one chocolate, one vanilla and one strawberry. The combination was abandoned when the price of strawberries rose, and 3 Musketeers became a giant, chocolate-flavored bar.

Learning the Ropes

Wanting to become an expert in chocolate, Forrest Mars traveled to Switzerland in 1933 and took an hourly wage as a factory worker. He first worked for Jean Tobler, who in 1899 introduced his famous Toblerone bar, and next got a job at the factory owned by Henri Nestlé, the chemist who invented milk chocolate together with Swiss candy maker Daniel Peter. These master chocolatiers unwittingly provided Forrest with a first-rate chocolate-manufacturing education.

DID YOU  KNOW?

Company patriarch Forrest Mars Sr. only granted one press interview in his lifetime in 1966.

Chocolate Spies

In the 1930s, it became common practice for chocolate companies to spy on one another. Candy makers in Europe began to hire detective agencies to investigate their employees and flush out the moles. There was so much industrial espionage that manufacturing processes were designated off-limits, and all businesses that dealt with candy makers were forced to sign confidentiality agreements.

Out of this World
Mars turned down Stephen Spielberg's request for M&Ms to be E.T.'s favorite candy, not realizing the incredible marketing potential this offer could provide.

DID YOU  KNOW?

Mars Inc. did not make any products with peanut butter until well into the 1990s. The reason? The Mars family doesn't eat peanut butter and reportedly despises it. Peanut butter M&Ms are the only peanut butter item in their repertoire.

Business Acumen

With its updated, cutting-edge machinery and equipment, Mars Inc. has always been an industry leader. It can afford to do this because Mars has never had any debt—and the family vows that it never will. Mars reinvests almost all of its profits into operations, and the Mars family rarely takes out dividends.

DID YOU  KNOW?

There were no red M&Ms produced between 1976 and 1987. Mars Inc. responded to consumer concern surrounding red food dye. Although the dye in question was never used by Mars, the company pulled the red candy from the bag. Red and yellow were the original M&M "spokes-candies." They were not available for comment.

Tropical Mars
Inspired by the drop in price of tropical fruit in the late 1930s, Forrest Mars introduced a pineapple version of the Mars Bar, which, not surprisingly, didn't last very long.

Changing Times

These days, Big Chocolate has come a long way from the paternalistic men who founded these companies. Secrecy, mistrust and fierce competition rule the industry, and the days of collaboration and camaraderie are long gone.

A MINER FOR A HEART OF COCOA

Domingo Ghirardelli

In 1849, Domingo Ghirardelli, a young Italian chocolatier, arrived in San Francisco in search of gold. He struck it rich in the form of chocolate, which he began selling, quite successfully, to miners.

Young Ghirardelli began his chocolate journey in Italy with an apprenticeship to a master chocolate chef at the age of 11. An adventurer, Ghirardelli set sail at the age of 20 and traveled the world, armed with his knowledge of fine chocolate making. Ambitious, young and hard working, he settled in Uruguay, but moved to Peru after only a year, where he opened up a small chocolate store.

Hearing word that western North America was the place to be, Ghirardelli sent his business partner to California with 600 pounds of chocolate in 1848. Two weeks later, gold was discovered, and the chocolate sold almost instantaneously. Ghirardelli joined his colleague in February 1849 to try his hand at panning for gold. Realizing he could make more money selling chocolate, he set up a chocolate shop. Despite two major fires in San Francisco that devastated both of Ghirardelli's stores and a Depression-era bankruptcy, the Ghirardelli Chocolate Company grew into a very successful enterprise and was later purchased by Lindt & Sprüngli in 1998.

More Chocolate Landmarks

1868: A Parisian named Étienne Guittard arrives in California and starts the Guittard Chocolate Company, which is still in operation.

1896: Fanny Farmer and her cookbook introduce the world to chocolate brownies.

1912: The Whitman's Company becomes one of the first companies to sell boxed chocolates in cellophane when it introduces the Whitman's Sampler with a guide to what's inside.

1922: Using Hershey's chocolate, H.B. Reese, a former Hershey employee, creates the Reese's Peanut Butter Cup. Hershey buys the recipe from Reese in 1963.

1923: Mr. and Mrs. Russell Stover open up a candy business in their bungalow in Denver, Colorado. The company is appropriately named Mrs. Stover's Bungalow Candies and, in 1954, becomes Russell Stover Candies. In 1993, Russell Stover buys Whitman's Chocolates for $35 million.

1930: Having run out of baking chocolate, Ruth Wakefield instead adds chunks of a Nestlé bar to her cookie dough. Owner of the Toll House Inn in New Bedford, Massachusetts, Wakefield has inadvertently created an American favorite, the chocolate chip cookie.

1938: The Nestlé Crunch is introduced. It is the first chocolate bar to combine milk chocolate and crunchy crisps to create a sensory eating experience that blends taste, texture and sound.

1939: Nestlé introduces the hallowed chocolate chip.

ČOKOLÁDA
in Czech

THE GANONGS: A CANADIAN SUCCESS STORY

The Ganong Brothers

St. Stephen, New Brunswick, is the self-declared "Capital of Chocolate." The Ganong brothers started their chocolate company in 1873, which today has the distinction of being the oldest family-owned candy business in Canada. It is a well-loved company, mostly because the Ganongs have remained true to their small-town roots by staying in the community and refusing to submit to the Maritime curse of selling up and shipping out.

The company from "down home" has been resilient and uncompromising and has persevered through fires, economic depression and huge changes. Surviving impending bankruptcy, countless buyout offers, heavy taxes and a fluctuating market, the Ganongs are a genuine Canadian success story.

Canada was only six years old when James and Gilbert Ganong founded the company in 1873. As has often been the story in chocolate making, neither man had aspirations of becoming a chocolate maker. In fact, James was a jockey in Chicago for a short period of time, and Gilbert was a teacher with hopes of someday going to medical school. Instead, the two ended up as grocers in a sleepy little town by the St. Croix River. Eventually, they decided to concentrate on confectionery and hired professional candy makers from Germany, Baltimore and Scotland.

The company later decided to focus on chocolate, which at the turn of the century was becoming the rage of the confectionery business. By patenting its hand-dipped chocolate process, providing bonuses to salesmen for selling GB chocolates and introducing the penny candy, Ganong prospered though the 1890s depression.

Penny Perfection
To keep their child consumers interested, Ganong introduced three new penny candy pieces every month and took three out of circulation. Overall, the company maintained about 150 kinds of penny candy at a time. With names like Dudes, Sunbeams and Zoo-Zoos, spending a penny was never so satisfying.

Rich Repertoire

At one point, Ganong produced as many as 1100 different types of chocolates and candies. Here are a few of the favorites:

- The Pal-o-mine bar, with its yellow-fudge and coconut center coated with chocolate peanuts, is one of the oldest continuously produced candy bars in North America.

- The Evangeline bar, invented in 1910, was the first chocolate nut bar and was named after the family's Jersey cow, who faithfully provided the milk.

- The Big Chief bar represented the public's fascination with Native Americans in the 1920s. Collector cards with pictures of different Native leaders, based on U.S. Department of the Interior portraits, were included inside the wrapper of each bar. There were 50 in all, and children, of course, were encouraged to collect the entire set. The Rodeo bars had a series of collector cards with a rodeo theme.

- Ganong was one of the first companies to sell boxed chocolates. The company's oldest brand, Delecto, has graced the Christmas tables of Canadians for 100 years. Considered the "premium chocolate" line, Delecto is still Canada's most popular box of assorted chocolates.

 "It wouldn't be Christmas without Chicken Bones." Only Maritimers understand that this line refers to Ganong's truly unique, pink-shaded candy. The unsweetened, chocolate center is covered with hard-boiled sugar and cinnamon and shaped somewhat like a chicken bone. The creation of candy maker Frank Sparhawk, Chicken Bones are a distinctive Maritime Christmas tradition.

Going Strong

Run today by a fifth-generation Ganong family member, the company has had to constantly reinvent itself to remain competitive. It now has the Canadian license to manufacture and distribute Sunkist products. They also make and package the majority of Laura Secord chocolates and assortments.

Joining the Family Business
Hand-dipping chocolates was a process that took a long time to learn and even longer to master. Eleanor Deacon became known as the fastest hand-dipper in the company's history. She would also go on to marry James Ganong's grandson, Whidden, in 1941 after a lightning-fast 14-year courtship.

 DID YOU KNOW?

In 1999, Ganong was named one of Canada's 50 best-managed companies.

MAKING SENSE OF THE TERMINOLOGY

Cacao Pod

The large fruit of the cacao tree, each pod measures up to 12 inches in length and contains about 50 seeds, which can be processed into chocolate. The pods are usually bright green while growing, and red, yellow or brown when ripe. The three main classifications of cacao varieties are Criollo, Forastero and Trinitario.

Cacao Beans

These are the seeds from the fruit pods of cacao trees and are encased in a sticky pulp within the pod. They are fermented, dried, roasted and ground to create chocolate.

Cacao Nibs

The heart of chocolate, the nibs are the interior meat of the cacao bean and are typically ground into a fine paste called cocoa liquor. Recipes sometimes call for cacao nibs as a garnish or use them to add a crunchy, subtle flavor to both savory and sweet dishes.

Chocolate Liquor

Unfortunately, chocolate liquor is not cacao with alcohol inside; rather, it is the gritty, bitter, raw product that remains after the cacao nibs are pressed. Also referred to as cocoa mass or essence, liquor is the base used in your favorite types of chocolate.

Cocoa Butter

The yellowish-white fat from the nibs.

CLASSIFYING COCOA BEANS

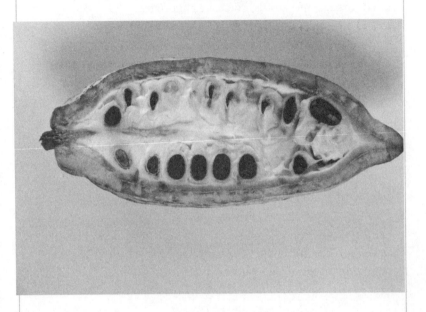

Geographical Classification

Central American cocoa (Mexico, Nicaragua and Costa Rica)
South American cocoa (Ecuador, Brazil, Venezuela)
West Indian cocoa (Trinidad and Tobago, Jamaica)
West African cocoa (Gold Coast countries, Togo, Cameroon, São Tomé)
East African cocoa (Malagasy)
Asian cocoa (Sri Lanka, Java, Indonesia)
Australian cocoa (Samoa)

Classification by Processing Stage

Raw, dried or roasted
Dried, roasted and cleaned
Broken
Cocoa mass
Chemically treated and processed cocoa mass
Broken beans containing up to 10 percent extraneous material
Bean particles obtained during processing
Cocoa shells

Classification by Bean Type

This is the most common of the three classification methods.
Read on to learn more about the beans.

CHOKOLADE
in Danish

CHOOSING THE BEAN

Criollo
Considered the Rolls Royce of cacao beans, Criollo means "native" and is the type of cacao the Mayans and Aztecs would have originally used. Cultivated in Venezuela, Belize and other parts of Central America, there are also plantations in Samoa (Polynesia), Sri Lanka, Madagascar and Java. Criollo seeds are milder, more aromatic and less bitter than other beans and therefore make for tastier chocolate. This variety is used in high-quality chocolate but rarely in its pure form. Production is extremely limited and only represents about 5 to 10 percent of worldwide production.

Forastero
Meaning "foreign," Forastero cacao originated in South America but today also comes from Ghana, Nigeria, the Ivory Coast, Sri Lanka, Malaysia and Indonesia. The plants are hardier and yield more beans in a shorter time, but produce below-average chocolate with a stronger and more bitter flavor. Most Forastero beans are used primarily for blending and account for about 85 percent of the world's production. The Arriba variety of Forastero grown in Ecuador is the exception. Comparable to a Criollo bean, Arriba is more delicate and aromatic than the majority of Forastero beans and has a great name.

Trinitero
Trinitero cacao is a hybrid of Criollo and Forastero and is cultivated primarily in the Caribbean. As the name suggests, it comes from Trinidad, where the Spaniards cultivated Criollo cacao in the 17th century. The Spanish tried to create varieties of cacao that produced more pods while still retaining some of the Criollo flavor. Trinitero cacao has a spicy, robust and

complex flavor and represents 10 to 15 percent of the world's production. It is used mainly for blending.

Cru

This name designates the highest quality cacao from selected plantations, each of which produces the best-quality chocolate that any connoisseur could desire. As with fine wines, many cru chocolates are considered "vintage" and have numbered bars. Cru chocolate is often named after the region from which the cacao beans are harvested. Among the varieties of cru are Madagascar, which has a distinctive almond aroma, the bitter and robust Ghana, and Trinidad, which is full-bodied and smells of chestnuts. Other cru varieties include Ecuador, Jamaica, Esmeraldas, Rio Caribe Superior and Sumatra.

CHOCOLADE
in Dutch

COCOA PRODUCTION

Processing vs. Manufacturing
Cocoa processing and chocolate manufacturing are two equally important but different processes. Cocoa processing converts the beans into liquor, whereas manufacturing includes blending and refining the cocoa liquor to make consumer products.

Other than choosing the bean quality, cocoa processing is the most important step in assuring quality chocolate. This process can be subdivided into eight phases.

Phase One: Harvest
The cacao pods, which grow on the trunk and the larger branches of the plant, are broken off in order to remove the beans enclosed in their moist and sticky pulp. The beans are piled up on banana leaves to make the fermentation process easier.

Phase Two: Fermentation
Lasting from four to six days, the fermentation process reduces the bitterness and the sharp, acidic flavor, developing the base for the aroma. The cacao beans are subjected to temperatures of up to 120°F, which melts the gummy pulp and creates chemical reactions inside the bean itself.

Phase Three: Drying
The cacao beans, now pulp-free, are dried, reducing their humidity to seven percent.

Phase Four: Roasting
The cacao beans enter the roaster whole and are heated to a temperature between 250 and 285°F. The roasting of the cacao is the most delicate step of the process, and knowing the ideal roasting point requires great experience. Improper roasting may have negative effects on the quality of the cocoa, which may end up with a burned flavor. The total roasting time depends on the type of beans and the quality.

Lower-quality beans are cooked more slowly, as they tend to be more bitter.

Phase Five: Winnowing
Once cooled, the beans are thrown into the winnowing machine, which separates the shells from the seed, or nib, inside. The shells go on to mulch makers or very low-grade "chocolate" companies.

Phase Six: Grinding
The cacao beans are ground using giant hydraulic presses that squeeze the cocoa butter out of the chocolate liquor. The pressed cake that remains can be cooled, pulverized and sifted into cocoa powder or mixed with sugar or milk. The chocolate is born!

Phase Seven: Conching
The chocolate is put into vats and mixed at a constant temperature for anywhere between 72 and 120 hours. Heavy rollers swirl continually through the mixture, developing the chocolate flavor. Swiss chocolatier Rudolfe Lindt is famous for inventing the conching process in 1880, utilizing shell-shaped rollers to grind the tiny chocolate particles. Often, cocoa butter is re-added to give the chocolate a smooth finish.

Phase Eight: Tempering
The chocolate is heated, cooled and reheated again in order to stabilize the cocoa butter crystals. This operation determines the chocolate's malleability, gloss and consistency. Liquid chocolate must stay within a precise temperature range in order to be properly tempered.

DIFFERENT TYPES OF CHOCOLATE

Milk Chocolate
Milk chocolate is made of at least 10 percent chocolate liquor and 12 percent milk solids, combined with sugar, cocoa butter and vanilla.

Sweet and Semisweet Chocolate
Sweet and semisweet chocolate both contain 15 to 35 percent chocolate liquor, cocoa butter, vanilla and sugar. There is no precise distinction between these two types of chocolate, and the two are commonly lumped together as "dark" or "plain."

Bittersweet and Bitter Chocolate
Bittersweet chocolate is made from 50 percent chocolate liquor. Bitter chocolate or unsweetened chocolate is simply hardened chocolate liquor or mass. It is used for baking and is therefore sometimes referred to as "baking chocolate" or "baker's chocolate."

White Chocolate
White chocolate is actually not chocolate at all. The ingredients are the same as those in milk chocolate but without the chocolate liquor. White chocolate is made from cocoa butter, which doesn't contain any of the taste or color of the cocoa bean. For this reason, white chocolate must legally be called "white confectionery coating."

So, What Makes Chocolate So Good, Anyway?
Great chocolate manufacturers choose their cacao beans in the same way a winemaker chooses grape varieties. Some prefer to buy beans; others favor chocolate mass. When being tasted,

fine chocolate should have a good balance between bitter and sweet, and a long complex finish that is comparable to a fine wine.

Chocolatiers vs. Chocolate Makers

It can be hard to distinguish the difference between a chocolatier and a chocolate maker. Because making chocolate is such a complicated and expensive process and requires such specific and artisanal knowledge and equipment, chocolate makers are rarer than people may realize. A chocolate maker buys and roasts cacao beans and grinds them into chocolate, while a chocolatier buys that chocolate, known as couverture, melts it down and uses it to create his own chocolate masterpieces.

Šokolaad
in Estonian

TASTING CHOCOLATE

Putting Chocolate to the Test

There is a difference between eating chocolate and tasting it. Tasting chocolate has nothing to do with inviting friends over to enjoy a decadent dessert with a glass of red wine. As previously outlined, there are many flavors that complement chocolate, but true connoisseurs say there's a technique and an art to the appreciation of "tasting" it.

Start With a Clean Palate

In order to truly capture the taste of high-quality chocolate, it's very important not to mix flavors. Sweet or bitter drinks such as coffee will cause taste buds to overload and alter the taste of the chocolate, making it tricky to enjoy its intricate flavors. Drinking something neutral such as water will cleanse your palate prior to tasting.

Take Your Time

Chocolate can be infused with a wide range of taste combinations. Different types of beans, spices and flavorings such as licorice, ginger, raspberry, cinnamon or chili peppers will yield diverse results. In order to truly enjoy the range, savor the flavor slowly. Solid chocolate does take longer to be absorbed by taste buds. If you gobble up the chocolate, most of the flavor will be lost. Chocolate melts at body temperature, so place a piece of chocolate on your tongue and let it melt slowly. Enjoying the velvety texture and allowing your palate to take in the full flavor will only enhance the experience.

Try Something New

Don't be afraid to branch out. If you are unfamiliar with the darker varieties of chocolate, start with milk chocolate and work your way up to stronger, more intense flavors. Have fun experimenting. The higher the concentration of chocolate, the lower the sugar content and, generally, the healthier it is. All the benefits of this magic bean can be unlocked as it slowly dissolves on your tongue.

SUKLAA
in Finnish

BECOMING AN EXPERT

A Five-Point Checklist

So now that you are ready, here are a few other things that may help you on your quest. According to thenibble.com, a great food-finds website, one examines five things in the exploration of chocolate: appearance, snap, aroma, mouth feel and taste. As with anything, becoming a chocolate expert requires a lot of knowledge and practice. There is a lot to master, but luckily, it is a pleasurable trip if you are up to the task.

1. Appearance
The chocolate should have an even, glossy surface. Lack of shine indicates staleness.

2. Snap
This term refers to the way the chocolate performs when broken from a bar. Good chocolate should make a crisp, clear sound. If it splinters, it is too dry; if it breaks reluctantly, it is too waxy.

3. Aroma
As with wine, there are hundreds of aromas associated with chocolate. Guides of chocolate descriptors are widely available to help you describe the scent. Expert tasters can even distinguish roast scent and can tell what kind of roast the beans underwent. For the beginner, just inhale the aroma of the bar and try to distinguish the different scents.

4. Mouth Feel
This somewhat unpoetic phrase is used by experts to mean texture. The "mouth feel" of chocolate can be dry, gritty, moist, waxy or smooth, depending mostly on how long the chocolate has been conched. If you don't like the mouth feel, it is likely more the style of chocolate that you don't like and not the chocolate itself.

5. Taste

There are three primary components of taste by which an authority will judge chocolate:

- Sweetness (determined by percentage of sugar)

- Chocolatitude (determined by percentage of chocolate liquor)

- Bouquet (determined by quality of beans, roasting time and blending formula)

What to Drink with Chocolate

In order to avoid confusing the taste buds, purists believe that only mineral water will do when it comes to tasting chocolate. For the less finicky, there are numerous wines and liqueurs that can be paired with chocolate, depending on the type. Mocha or raspberry liqueur with dark chocolate can be delightful, as can a nice glass of champagne, port or a variety of dessert wines. Brandy would complement milk chocolate, but not dark.

White milk and milk chocolate are a dynamic duo and a long-standing childhood favorite that can't be beat. If you're looking for a beer to drink with chocolate, you would do well with a strong Belgian ale or a flavored cherry ale.

And, of course, tea and coffee are always stalwart companions, as long as you follow the golden rule of pairing sweet with savory. Combine dark chocolate with sweeter teas and coffees, and sweet chocolates with stronger flavors.

STORING CHOCOLATE

The best place to store chocolate is in your mouth.
                                                    –Clay Gordon

Best to Eat It Right Away

Ideally, you want to eat chocolate within a day or two of its
being made for maximum enjoyment. That means that the best
place to buy chocolate is at a chocolaterie. If you can't possibly
polish off that last square of chocolate and storage is necessary,
here is what you need to know about storing it.

Well, If the Experts Insist...

Although chocolatiers routinely refrigerate or freeze their
chocolates as an alternative to adding preservatives, chocolate
connoisseur Clay Gordon insists that for the person at home,
refrigerating or freezing chocolate should be considered a last
resort. There is a direct correlation between freshness and quality.

Finicky Fare

Heat, humidity and odor are the enemies of chocolate. If chocolate is too warm, then obviously it will melt or burn. If it is too
cold or brought too quickly to room temperature, it will sweat
like yo' mama at the gym. This makes chocolate the Goldilocks
of the food world. At warm temperatures, chocolate may
"bloom," which means that the cocoa butter rises to the surface
and produces a whitish film. Sugar bloom occurs when moisture
condensing on the surface forms a layer of sugar crystals, making the chocolate gritty and permanently ruining its texture.

For short-term storage, a cool, dry place is *juuust* right for this
fastidious princess. Connoisseurs use a wine cellar or wine
fridge, but if you don't own one or for storing chocolate for
longer periods of time, it is best wrapped in paper towel and

stored in a resealable plastic bag or container in your freezer. Avoid aluminum and plastic wrap.

Unless you want to eat chocolate that tastes like onion, fridge storage is not recommended, since cocoa butter soaks up odors rapidly.

No matter the case, it is important to take your time when bringing chocolate back to life. From the freezer, leave the bags of chocolate in your fridge overnight or for at least eight to twelve hours. From the refrigerator, place the bags in a cool, dark place and let them warm to room temperature for one to two hours.

Under optimal conditions, dark chocolate can be kept for up to three years, though whoever has the fortitude to test out that theory can't, in good conscience, call themselves a chocoholic. Milk chocolate can be stored for up to one year and white chocolate for no more than eight months.

Need a Reason to Buy Good-Quality Chocolate?

Have a hard time justifying the extra expense? This may tip the scales, so to speak. Quality chocolate contains half the sugar of mass-produced milk chocolate, which is comprised of 65 percent sugar, 20 percent milk solids and 3 percent vegetable fat. Cheaper chocolate actually only contains 11 percent cocoa, while quality chocolate contains 56 percent. Also, some chocolate companies use the rejected husks of cacao nibs after winnowing to make low-grade chocolate.

The Top 10 Chocolate Bars

According to seventypercent.com, these are the best chocolate bars and the companies that make them:

Company	Name of Bar
1. Amedei	Chuao
2. Michel Cluizel 1er Cru de Plantation Vila	Gracinda
3. Amedei	Madagascar
4. Pralus	Le 100%
5. Michel Cluizel	Hacienda "Los Anconès"
6. Guittard	L'Harmonie
7. Domori	Ecuador
8. Domori	Chacao Absolute
9. Domori	Puertomar
10. Felchlin	Cru Sauvage

Chocolat
in French

TRADITIONS RELATED TO CHOCOLATE

Mexico: Day of the Dead

While North American children are trick-or-treating and celebrating Halloween, Mexico is beginning its celebration of *El Día de los Muertos* (Day of the Dead). The holiday commemorates All Saints' Day and All Souls' Day (November 1 and 2) and is a time during which the living remember the dead.

Mexicans visit the graves of their loved ones and leave offerings of food and drink, hoping for a visit from the departed, whom they believe are temporarily reborn at this time. In homes, ornate altars are adorned with pictures and provisions, including hot chocolate, chicken with chocolate mole sauce and chocolate skulls inscribed on the forehead with the names of departed relatives. Some believe that the visiting spirits of the deceased eat the spirit of the food, so friends and relatives eat the offerings as a tribute to the dead.

In Mexico, although hot chocolate is never served at funerals, everyone drinks it on the Day of the Dead. There are still many present-day cultural associations between cacao and fertility and regeneration. Hot chocolate is a symbol of human blood, much like wine in Christianity.

St. Lucia: Fantasy Island

If sailing and chocolate float your boat, then a trip to St. Lucia may be just the ticket. The Fond Doux Holiday Plantation is a colonial estate that gives tours and is one of the many places to learn everything you ever wanted to know about growing cacao.

Fond Doux received some notoriety in March 2008 when Prince Charles visited the estate with his wife, Camilla, the Duchess of Cornwall. He was there as part of a five-island Caribbean tour, and besides sampling some of the local chocolate, he also broke ground for a new cocoa factory at a nearby cacao estate.

Wishing to show their support for the environment and reduce their carbon footprint, the royal couple opted to sail rather than fly and toured the islands aboard a 246-foot mega-yacht, complete with hot tub, gym and 24-member crew.

For us commoners, chocolate sailing packages that stop at St. Lucia and other islands within the area are also available and offer an alternative for passengers who prefer not to travel on the big cruise ships.

Bolivia: That'll Chicha!

The Bolivian capital of La Paz is the highest capital city in the world at 11,811 feet above sea level. The city is known as the "Shanghai of the Americas" for its unique markets, traditional customs and high-altitude location. It's also a popular location for golfers because the thin air helps the ball travel farther. Butch Cassidy and the Sundance Kid died in Bolivia; so did Che Guevara. It is alleged that around 1870, a British ambassador was publicly humiliated by a General Melgarejo, who stripped him naked, strapped him to a donkey, forced him to drink a barrelful of chocolate and then paraded him and the mule around the Witches' Market—all because the poor ambassador declined an offer to drink the local fermented wheat beverage called chicha. An infuriated Queen Victoria declared that Bolivia didn't exist and literally crossed it off all British-made maps.

A quaint Argentinean bar in Copacabana serves a deadly concoction known as the Tatu Correta milkshake, which contains milk, eggs, chocolate and cognac. Light on the milk, heavy on the cognac, you'll feel the effects of this drink faster than you can say "Lake Titicaca."

Sucre is considered Bolivia's chocolate capital. Quinoa (pronounced *KEEN-whah*) is a high-energy grain native to the high valleys of the Andes. Containing up to 50 percent more protein than most other grains, it is called the "mother grain" by the Inca. In Bolivia and Peru, chocolate and quinoa are frequently paired. Like tofu, quinoa soaks up the taste of whatever it is cooked with.

Venezuelan Party Food
It is said that it is not a true Venezuelan party without *tequeños*—small rolls filled with hot cheese or chocolate. The name originates from Los Teques, a city just outside Caracas.

Italy: Sicilian Chocolate

In January 1693, a terrible earthquake devastated the Sicilian town of Modica and killed 2400 people. Despite the destruction, certain traditions survived unscathed. One of them was preparing bitter chocolate and using it in savory cuisine. Residents in Modica eat a traditional chocolate dish known as *'mpanatigghi*, which are little pastries stuffed with minced meat and chocolate. *Liccumie*, a variant stuffed with eggplant and chocolate, is also very popular. Other varieties are made with local marzipan, grated lemon rind and vanilla.

Malta: Carnival Cake

In Malta, the only time that chocolate is eaten is in February at Carnival time. The Maltese *prinjolata*, or carnival cake, is a traditional favorite.

Germany: Chocowurst

Fire up the barbecue. In 2005, chef Joerg Staroske won first prize at the Annual Sausage Championships in Berlin. His winning recipe? A chocolate sausage. The annual *Bratwurstmeisterschaft* invites Germany's top butchers to display their creations and compete for the prize of *Bratwurstmeister*. Staroske describes the taste of the sausage, which has orange peel as well as chocolate fragments, as "surprisingly different." No kidding.

Readers will be glad to know that some chocolate sausage recipes have no meat in them at all and so likely have more mass appeal. One recipe combines a mixture of white grapes, prunes, chocolate and Armagnac liqueur, which is then rolled into little loaves, covered in dark chocolate and rolled again in powdered sugar.

Austria: The Sachertorte

In 1832, Prince Klemens von Metternich sent orders to his kitchen to create a new cake. Legend has it that the head chef was sick, so the request created bedlam among the panic-stricken team of cooks. A 16-year-old apprentice cook named Franz Sacher got to work, using whatever ingredients were available in the kitchen, and created what would become probably the most famous chocolate cake of all time. Sacher presented the prince with two layers of dense, semisweet chocolate sponge cake separated by a fine layer of apricot jelly and covered with boiled sugar syrup icing called fondant. Known from then on as the Sachertorte, it has since become a classic Austrian dessert, and today, every coffee house in Vienna boasts its own version.

Bulgaria: Sweet Treat
Bulgarians enjoy eating *garash*, a cake made of ground walnuts and frosted with chocolate icing.

Estonia: Kamatahvel

A product unique to Estonia is the *kama* "chocolate" bar. *Kama* is a mixture of peas, rye, barley and wheat boiled in salted water and then sun-dried, oven-roasted and ground before being mixed with sour or curdled milk.

During the Cold War, chocolate was scarce in the Soviet Union because of the high price of cacao beans. Kalev, the country's main chocolate supplier, began replacing cocoa flour with *kama* flour. The resulting product not only tasted good but was cheaper than traditional chocolate bars and became very popular in Estonia.

With the fall of communism in the early 1990s, chocolate scarcity was no longer an issue, and consumers were suddenly surrounded by chocolate from around the world. Kalev discontinued the *kama* bar, probably feeling that it no longer had commercial appeal.

However, in 2001, the bar was reintroduced under the new name *Kamatahvel*. Stricter European Union regulations meant that Kalev could no longer claim that the bar was chocolate. There was no advertising campaign whatsoever, but demand was high enough that within months the newly introduced *Kamatahvel* was one of the top-selling "chocolate" bars on the market.

Have Some Halva

In the Middle East, halva is a popular dessert, though it varies slightly from country to country. Halva is usually made with flour, butter, sugar and chocolate, but there are many variations. A white halva, for example, is made with vanilla and sugar. Albanians also enjoy halva, which is usually sweet and eaten as a dessert at the end of a meal. Many stores all over Albania sell this popular creamy treat in large, fresh, inexpensive blocks that melt in your mouth.

Syria: Chocolate Parting Gifts

Most Syrians still follow old customs when it comes to celebrating births. Traditionally, on the fifth and sixth days following the birth of a child, the child's family holds a reception called a *mubarakeh* for relatives and friends.

At a *mubarakeh*, guests bring gifts of jewelry or clothing for either mother or infant. At these receptions, the hosts serve all kinds of traditional Syrian desserts or gelato. Women drink coffee, eat, gossip and dance for hours. As guests are leaving, chocolate, sugar-coated almonds and *man wa salwa*, or nougat, are given out.

Today, Syrians still follow the tradition, but the mother is no longer expected to host hundreds of women on the fifth and sixth days after the birth of her child. It is now acceptable for her to wait until she regains her strength.

India: Diwali Diya

Diwali is a festival of color, crackers, clothes and celebration! Taking its name from the symbolic *diyas*, clay lamps filled with oil and lit, the Festival of Lights is one of the most celebrated Hindu religious festivals. Spanning five days in late October and early November, Diwali is a time of renewal and marks a new moon and a new year of business. Honoring Lakshmi Pooja, the goddess of wealth and good fortune, Hindus take time to feast, shop, exchange gifts, wear new clothes and spend time with loved ones. *Rangolis*—intricate designs made with colored powder—decorate the main entrances of homes to greet the new year. Debts are paid off, homes are cleaned, and food—including chocolate—is eaten.

Besides a dizzying array of sweets, molded chocolate *diyas*, filled with jam and decorated with chocolate buttons and flakes, are consumed. Fudgy *diyas*, chocolate cereal *diyas*, creamy hot chocolate and boxes of European chocolates are all examples of things that are exchanged or gifted.

Pepero Day

November 11 is Pepero Day in both North and South Korea, when couples give each other chocolate-covered pretzel sticks called "Pepero," similar to Pocky.

The Philippines

The arm of the Spanish was very far-reaching and is responsible for a modern-day drink with ancient roots.

In the Philippines, a former Spanish colony, cacao is peeled, roasted and ground using the same instrument employed by the Maya. A *metate*, or grinding stone, is used to shape the unsweetened round tablets called *tableya*, to which ground peanuts are sometimes added for flavor. The *tableya* are then used to make Filipino treats such as *sikwate* and *champorado*.

Sikwate is a hot chocolate drink, which is also called *tsokolate*. *Champorado* is a hot, thick, sweet chocolate rice porridge. *Puto mayo*, made from sticky white rice, resembles what we know as a rice cake, and *budbod kabog* is a roll of steamed, sticky, white rice cooked with coconut milk and ginger and wrapped in banana leaves. *Sikwate* paired with sweet mangoes and *puto* or *budbod* is a favorite morning treat in the Philippines. Some Filipinos also enjoy *champorado* with salted fish.

No Chocolate in China

In China, a suitor trying to win a girl's heart needs to first pay a visit to the family and have dinner. And showing up with a box of chocolates or a bouquet of flowers won't go over well, either. The Chinese are not traditionally chocolate eaters. For a young man trying to win his girlfriend's parents over, offering a bag of fruit is the standard and probably best way to go.

Japan: *Barentain Dei*

Japanese women in don't wait around on Valentine's Day expecting chocolates or flowers or romantic candle-lit dinners from the men in their lives. In Japan, it is customary for the women to be the gift-givers. On Valentine's Day, called *Barentain Dei*, gifts are offered to boyfriends and husbands. *Giri-choco*, or "obligation chocolate," is given to male co-workers, bosses, classmates and friends to whom a woman has no romantic attachment. About 80 percent of Japanese women participate in the tradition, which generates a total revenue of over $400 million countrywide on the holiday.

All this female kindness is not in vain, though. One month later, on March 14, Japan, Korea and Taiwan celebrate White Day, when it is the men's turn to reciprocate their affection with gifts that vary from chocolate to expensive jewelry.

CLOSER TO HOME: CHOCOLATE IN THE UNITED STATES AND CANADA

Louisiana: French Quarter Treat

Pralines were invented by a 17th-century cook for his master, Count César du Plessis-Praslin. Originally, pralines were simply almonds coated with boiled sugar, and legend has it that Count Praslin used them to woo the ladies, though there is also some speculation that pralines were used as a digestive aid.

New Orleans is famous for its fresh pralines. The recipe was brought to Louisiana, where both nuts and sugarcane were widely available, from France in the 18th century. Over time, the recipe was adjusted to appeal to the rich appetites of the New Orleanais—cream was added, as was butter and brown sugar. The almonds were replaced with less-expensive local pecans, and a tradition was born.

Many other praline varieties now exist, including caramel, coconut, rum, vanilla, chocolate, peanut butter and piña colada. One of the most unusual variations is a praline garlic sundae, flavored with bourbon and roasted, caramelized garlic.

DID YOU KNOW?

In the early 1900s, pralines were a means for free women of color to make money in New Orleans. Older black women, called *pralinières*, sold pralines in the streets of the French Quarter.

To Do Before You Die

Locals say there is nothing better than a hot, fresh praline right off the marble slab in New Orleans. The fresher, the better. They are never made with preservatives, so they only last about a week. Even though the praline cools quickly, the pecan inside retains its warmth, and the two combined are an opus of nut and sugar, hot and cool—sweet perfection.

If you visit Louisiana, be prepared to ask for these sweet treats in the local tongue. The proper pronunciation is *prah-lean*, while the name of the nut itself is pronounced by the rather rude-sounding *peck-on*. Visitors looking for *pray-leans* may be directed towards a church, where they can talk to God while standing against a pew.

New York: Home of the Egg Cream

Milk, seltzer and chocolate syrup—the making of a delicious drink? Not to be confused with a Creme Egg, the New York egg cream is a drink of culinary lore.

Lou Reed sang about it; Elliot Willensky wrote about it. But the New York egg cream was made famous in Brooklyn, where all old-time candy stores used to have soda fountains. Originally used to fatten up skinny Brooklyn immigrant kids from Europe at the turn of the last century, the egg cream did indeed contain an egg white, along with equal parts real cream and seltzer and a touch of chocolate sauce to taste. During the Depression, the cream was replaced with milk, and the egg white was left out, and these days, the recipe contains neither egg nor cream.

There are several stories and legends about the origin of the chocolate egg cream.

Some believe it appeared in New York in the 1880s. After tasting a similar drink called chocolat et crème in Paris, France, teenage Yiddish-theater star Boris Thomashevsky asked to have one made in New York.

Another popular theory is that the egg cream was created in 1890 by Jewish candy-store owner Louis Auster in Brooklyn, New York. Auster could barely keep up with the demand for his popular drink and was approached by a national ice cream chain to buy the recipe. When Auster refused their low bid, one of the executives threw an anti-Semitic slur at him. Auster was understandably incensed and vowed to take his egg cream recipe to the grave with him. To this day, the formula has remained a closely guarded secret, and surviving family members have respected Auster's wishes, never publicly revealing the secret to his success.

Devotees say that a perfect egg cream has a good head on it and is best when enjoyed immediately, otherwise it loses its fizz. The drink is popular partly because it tastes so surprisingly fantastic and partly because it is nearly impossible to mass-produce—the cream, chocolate and soda have a tendency to separate and go bad after a couple days, so efforts to pasteurize or preserve the product ruin the taste.

Either way, this drink may be another one of those quirky cultural phenomena that just can't be explained to those who didn't grow up with it. Just like tasting a praline in New Orleans, sampling a New York egg cream may be one of those things to add to your Bucket List.

Kentucky: 100-Proof Chocolate?
Would a visit to Kentucky be complete without loading up on 100-proof bourbon? Originally a drink, Kentucky Colonels were turned into chocolates with a kick in 1919 by Ruth Booe.

Nevada: The World's Largest Chocolate Fountain

Designed by Montreal artist Michel Mailhot, the floor-to-ceiling chocolate fountain at the Bellagio Hotel in Las Vegas is a sight to behold! This visually stunning masterpiece is the first of its kind and holds the title as the world's tallest and largest-volume chocolate fountain. The fountain took two years of engineering, planning and design by a team of experts.

Six pumps circulate close to two tons of melted white, medium and dark chocolate, while six ceiling spouts disburse the sweet confection into 25 handcrafted artistic glass vessels. Boasting over 500 feet of stainless-steel piping, the fountain stands 27 feet tall, 14 of which is visible to the public.

Want to reach out and touch it? Too bad. The fountain is surrounded by 300 pounds of glass panels.

Not for Eating

The fountain works like a regular water fountain and was designed to operate 24 hours a day for over a year without having to change or replace the chocolate. Since each of the three types of chocolate behaves very differently, pipes with different amounts of flowing hot oil keep the chocolate thinned. Since chocolate contains no water, there's no evaporation. Basically, it's a fat fountain.

Canada: Land of Chocolate Romance

From one end of the country to the next, it turns out that Canadians are pretty romantic. The pursuit of chocolate can take one from the tops of the Malahat mountain pass north of Victoria in British Columbia to the rolling hills of the Laurentians in Quebec. Either way, the pursuit of chocolate is alive and well.

Pay attention gentlemen—suitors looking to betroth their loved ones can do it in style with a new experience offered in Victoria on Vancouver Island, British Columbia. Three Canadian companies have done all the legwork and wrapped up a "Perfect Proposal" package for you and will let you take all the credit. The romantic getaway includes a custom-designed diamond ring, a weekend at one of the island's most breathtaking mountain resorts and, of course, a boatload of chocolates.

A man has two full nights to woo his lady with a dozen long-stemmed red roses, a bottle of Pacific Northwest sparkling wine, a fruit basket and chocolate truffles. If that doesn't get her in the mood, there is also a five-course dinner for two, a breakfast hamper and a full breakfast in the resort's dining room.

The celebration wouldn't be complete without a decadent evening of chocolate and champagne. The package also includes an intimate party for two in the Bernard Callebaut candy store. There's also a bottle of BC's best champagne or ice wine, as well as dessert liqueurs, which are paired with every variety of chocolate.

Couples will also leave with a champagne bottle filled with the world's best chocolate.

The newly engaged lucky lady might be feeling woozy from all the romance, but "I do" believe she'll say yes.

Bonjour Quebec

Quebec—land of maple sugar and sugar pies. Is it any surprise that it is also home to some delicious chocolate?

The town of Charlevoix is known for some of the best hand-made chocolates in the country. Fifty years ago, it was still very common to make and dip chocolates by hand, though with mechanization, the technique has become rare. Residents and tourists alike do their best to enjoy the old-fashioned ways of the region.

The Charlevoix Gastronomic Feast, known as *La Fête des Saveurs*, is the icing on the cake of a beautiful 90-minute drive though the countryside east of Quebec City. Held in April, the feast is an annual fundraising event, and many of the chocolateries of the region participate, much to the delight of locals and tourists alike.

You will have ample time to recover before heading north to Jonquière, where for three days in August there is a similar festival. Featuring artists and producers from the area, chocolate buffs may want to check out this small-town festival. Beer and sausage, singers and chocolate, plus all the ambiance you can handle.

DIE SCHOKOLADE
in German

CHOCOLATE DRINKS FROM AROUND THE WORLD

Bored of the same old thing? Chocolate is a well-traveled confection. Almost every country has added its own unique twist on its preparation. Likewise, certain cities and countries have their own versions of chocolate drinks, both hot and cold.

Vienna, Austria

Flavored with sugar and vanilla, topped with heaps of whipped cream and sprinkled with cocoa powder—a trip to Vienna would not be complete without sampling a delicious cup of this rich hot chocolate, for which the city is famous.

Arriving in Austria in about 1640, hot chocolate was almost certainly spread throughout the Holy Roman Empire by the international network of monasteries and convents. Charles VI introduced chocolate to his court in Vienna in 1713 after a visit to Spain. The rest is delicious, frothy history.

England

This beverage resembles iced tea, only with cocoa added. First, prepare a pot of tea. Dissolve four teaspoons of cocoa in three cups of milk, adding the cocoa gradually, and then add seven (yes, that's right!) teaspoons of sugar. Mix the cocoa and tea together and pour over ice. Serves four.

Brazil

Dissolve several teaspoons of cocoa powder in half a cup of strong, hot coffee, and heat the mixture until it boils. Add three cups of boiling milk and mix vigorously. Fill a pan half full with hot water and leave the drink in the hot water for 10 minutes (this is called a *bain-marie*). Serve topped with whipped cream. Serves four.

Switzerland

To make one serving of this Swiss specialty, dissolve a teaspoon of cocoa powder in half a cup of milk. Once the mixture is well blended, add another half-cup of milk. Add a teaspoon of cream and stir well before serving.

Mexico

Melt four ounces of unsweetened chocolate in a double boiler. In a separate saucepan, heat four cups of milk with two cups of cream. Once heated, add three tablespoons to the chocolate and mix well. Add the rest of the milk mixture along with half a cup of sugar and one and a half teaspoons of cinnamon. In a separate bowl, combine two eggs and three teaspoons of vanilla. Add a tablespoon of chocolate mixture to the eggs and beat slowly.

Incorporate the rest of the egg mixture into the chocolate. Add a tiny piece of lemon peel. In a separate bowl, bring the mixture to a boil in the double boiler for three minutes and serve very hot.

Syracuse, Sicily

Melt a medium-sized bar of plain chocolate with a half cup of water and two teaspoons of condensed milk. Stir until it becomes a thin cream, and then add two teaspoons of brandy and two teaspoons of gin. When the mixture has cooled, add four table-spoons of orange juice. Mix well and refrigerate. Serve over ice.

Milan, Spain

This famous old drink known as *barbajada* was invented, it is said, by a theater impresario named Barbaja. To make it, com-bine three small cups of hot chocolate, three small cups of milk and three small cups of espresso in a double-boiler. Heat the chocolate, milk and espresso, stirring constantly. When a white foam appears around the surface, pour the *barbajada* into a cup and serve immediately. In the summer, this drink is best served cold.

EASTER EXTRAVAGANZA

It would be impossible to talk about chocolate celebrations around the world without addressing Christmas and Easter, the two most important worldwide celebrations.

Easter Bunny History

The hare and the rabbit have long been considered the most fertile animals and have always represented springtime and rebirth. During the Middle Ages, the rabbit became associated with chicken eggs, which were also a symbol of fertility. The court of Louis XV of France had already come up with the idea of covering an egg with chocolate, but another two centuries would pass before people tasted an egg made entirely of chocolate.

Oschter Haws

Chocolate Easter bunnies arrived in America with German settlers in the 1700s. For the children of the Pennsylvania Dutch, only a visit from Christkindel on Christmas Eve could rival the splendor of a visit from "Oschter Haws." Children believed that if they were good, Oschter Haws would actually lay a nest of magically colored eggs. No word on what he left for bad children, though it was likely less appetizing than a chocolate egg.

In anticipation of a visit from Oschter Haws, children would build nests in a private place in the home, barn or garden. Boys used their caps and girls their bonnets to make the nests. Eventually, Easter baskets replaced the caps and bonnets and became the most popular place to hide the holiday candies.

Early Easter Treats

The first edible Easter bunnies appeared in Germany in the early 1800s but were made with pastry and sugar. Together with gummy candies shaped like eggs, a primitive version of the jellybean, they were placed in straw nests and hidden around the house or garden for children to find. The custom changed over time, and eventually the Easter Bunny began to deposit eggs in children's shoes.

DID YOU KNOW?

The world's largest chocolate Easter egg sculpture took eight days, 50,000 Guylian praline chocolate bars and 26 master chocolate makers from the Guylian chocolaterie to complete. Measuring 27 feet, 3 inches long, 21 feet wide and weighing in at a hefty 4299 pounds, this egg is the heavyweight champion of the world and the Guinness World Record holder.

Wascally Wabbit Not Welcome Down Under

Instead of the Easter Bunny, Australians have an Easter Bilby. Europeans brought rabbits with them when they first settled in Australia, and the creatures promptly lived up to their rabbit reputations by reproducing rapidly. Eventually, there were so many rabbits that they became a problem for the native plants and animals of the country.

Enter *Billy the Aussie Easter Bilby!* This 1979 novel penned by an Australian author was the first to propose that the endangered animal take the place of the Easter Bunny, simultaneously raising awareness about the plight of the bilby. Since then, the idea of adopting the bilby as the Easter icon has hopped through the entire country.

In some schools, actual ceremonies are performed in which the Easter Bunny officially hands over the Easter reins to the bilby, announces his retirement and hangs up his basket. In an effort to embrace the new custom and get the entire nation behind the bilby, many supermarkets donate the proceeds from their chocolate bilby sales to protecting the endangered animal. Purchasing chocolate bilbies certainly seems like the yummiest solution to that problem. In 2003, chocolate bilbies outsold bunnies by eight to one.

The bilby does resemble the Easter Bunny in one way—it has long ears. Curiously, though, the bilby (or rabbit-eared bandicoot) has an upside-down pouch, which begs the important question: how does the bilby keep its eggs in there?

Belgium: Not for Chickens
Today, Belgium is known as one of the world leaders in chocolate making, but in the 1950s, chocolate Easter bunnies were unheard of. Chocolate fish eggs symbolized Easter, but store windows were often filled with real live baby chicks! Sadly, though some survived, most never made it to the end of Easter. Luckily, in the early 1960s, the practice was abandoned, and the little yellow chicks were replaced with equally adorable—but artificial—ones. Shortly afterwards, the Easter Bunny made his appearance, and the practice of gifting chocolate eggs, bunnies and bells became common practice.

Chocolate Spread for Passover

Matza, or *matzo*, is a hard, flat bread that resembles a cracker. It is served during the Jewish holiday of Passover, when eating leavened bread is forbidden. The feast itself is called the "Feast of the Unleavened Bread," and *matza* is the symbol of this important holiday.

What do you put on *matza*? The possibilities are endless, but everyone's childhood favorite is chocolate spread. Hashahar is the Israeli company responsible for this classic combo. When candy imports increased in the 1980s, Hashahar decided to abandon most of its candies and sweets and concentrate on producing its most popular item, chocolate spread. Today, the plant also makes baking chocolate and cocoa powder, but chocolate spread is (ahem) their "bread and butter."

DID YOU KNOW?

Hashahar's chocolate spread is available in three flavors: classic dairy, parve (containing neither meat nor dairy ingredients) and nut. Even though chocolate spread originated in Europe, hazelnut spread is more popular there. However, according to the Israeli company, the bitter parve spread is the one for true chocolate lovers.

Slovakia: Red Monday

Easter, known as *Velikonoce* or "Great Nights," is a very important celebration both in the Czech Republic and Slovakia. In Slovakia, there is a rather curious Easter Monday tradition wherein the men go around whipping the ladies and pouring water over them.

Throughout the day, groups of men visit their female relatives and friends demanding "treats," which can range from liquor or chocolate eggs to a peck on the cheek, and then the men spank the women with special whips. Made from braided willow branches, the whips have decorative ribbons on the end. In the past, it was common for women to add their own ribbons so the whip would indicate how many women that particular man had already visited.

If the women decide to make it interesting or play along, they will allow the men to chase them around. Otherwise, they just stand motionless, and the male visitors spank their bottoms. Willow branches are used because they are a symbol of spring. According to folk tradition, the fertility and vitality of the branches are believed to be transferred to the women during the whipping.

Easter Monday also involves dousing. Water is the symbol of life, and the pouring of water is a gesture meant to encourage vigor and health in the year ahead. Being "watered" can range from having a teaspoon of warm tap water dribbled over your head to having a bucket of frigid well water thrown at you. Women in cities also sometimes get sprayed with perfume, while those in villages get pitched into the river.

So let's review: the women get watered and whipped while the men get fed and given drinks, and the little boys are given money or chocolate.

Understandably, this tradition is enjoyed considerably more by the men than the women, though this wasn't always the case. Traditionally, in each village, the watering and whipping would be done by a group of single young men, who would decide among themselves which single young women they would visit. If the group left out a particular girl, it was a sign that none of the boys had any interest in her. Therefore, some people say that girls actually wanted to get watered and whipped. Who is willing to bet that a man made up the tradition *and* the story behind it.

CHOCOLATE FOR CHRISTMAS

Holland: The Feast of Sinterklaas

The Feast of Sinterklaas, celebrated on December 5, is an annual event that has been uniquely Dutch and Flemish for centuries. St. Nicholas' feast day, December 6, is observed in most Roman Catholic countries primarily as a feast for small children. But it is only in the Netherlands that the eve of his feast day (December 5) is celebrated nationwide by young and old, Christian and non-Christian, without any religious overtones.

All Dutch children know that Sinterklaas—or Santa Claus—lives in Spain. On December 5, most businesses close a bit early, and everyone heads home for dinner. Large chocolate letters—the first initial of each person's name—serve as place settings.

At many Dutch parties, the very last surprise in Sinterklaas' special burlap sack is a chocolate initial. They are handed out to everyone, starting with the youngest child. Chocolate initials are sometimes also left in shoes as Sinterklaas makes his nightly rounds, checking on children.

The "Initial" Origin

The custom of edible letters goes back to Germanic times when, at birth, children were given a letter made of bread as a symbol of good fortune. Convent schools in the Middle Ages used bread letters to teach the alphabet. When the letter was learned and could be written well, the pupil could eat up the bread letter. What an incentive!

Chocolate eventually replaced the bread dough. Today, the Dutch company Droste produces more than 20 million chocolate letters and de Heer another 10 million. In 2007, fair-trade chocolate letters were introduced by Oxfam, which provides a fair return to cacao growers and uses chocolate that has been produced without using child slave labor.

Can I Buy a Vowel?

Manufacturers keep track of the most popular chocolate letters and use sales to determine how many of each letter to make. In Holland, the best seller is *M*. Not only is it a popular letter for names, it can also be used for mama and *moeder*, or mother. *S* is the second most popular letter because it stands for Sinterklaas and can be used in a pinch if no others are available. Employers will often gift an *S* to employees. *P* for papa is also popular, while *O* and *V* are the least-popular letters. Most companies don't make *Q, U, X, Y* or *Z*.

Some consumers believe that the *M* and *W* look the biggest, especially compared with a letter like *I*, but all the letters weigh the same. In order to use the same amount of chocolate for each letter, the chocolate companies vary the thickness or the depth of the grooves in the letter. This way, one letter is not favored over another.

In 2001, as a result of a petition with 2700 signatures, a large supermarket chain in Holland promised to wait until 14 days before Sinterklaas' official mid-November arrival to begin selling chocolate letters. Parents didn't want their children singing Sinterklaas songs and getting excited in September.

Consumers excited about post-Sinterklaas chocolate-letter shopping sprees will be disappointed. In the Netherlands, the letters never go on sale. They disappear as quickly as Sinterklaas—any extras are sent back to the factory. What happens to them, only the chocolate makers know, but savvy chocolate connoisseurs may recognize the familiar flavor in their chocolate eggs and rabbits at Easter.

Here Comes Chanukah!
So Much Funukah!

Chanukah or Hanukkah is the Jewish Festival of Lights, often celebrated at about the same time as Christmas. It dates back to two centuries before the beginning of Christianity. The eight-day Jewish holiday celebrates a military victory and the miracle of the temple oil that lasted eight days instead of one.

Gelt is the Yiddish term for money. Modern day *gelt* includes saving bonds, checks and, more importantly to children, chocolate coins wrapped in gold foil. It has become a tradition to eat chocolate *gelt* during Chanukah. Initially, real coins were given. It is believed that in the late 18th and early 19th centuries, when Jews figured prominently in chocolate manufacturing, chocolate coins were fabricated to allow poor children to take part in the growing Jewish tradition of receiving *gelt* at Chanukah.

Others suggest that chocolate coins were a post–World War II invention, coinciding with Chanukah rising to the challenge of Christmas. Jews traditionally gave presents on Purim, not on Chanukah. Some believe that the shift was a clear reaction to the ubiquitous supremacy of Christmas.

"Dreidel, Dreidel, Dreidel…"

It is also customary to play games at Chanukah. The most common game uses a dreidel, a spinning top with a different Hebrew letter inscribed on each of its four sides. The stakes are usually high—chocolate coins. But sometimes pennies, peanuts or raisins are used. Each player puts a coin in the pot and takes turns spinning the dreidel. The letter on which the dreidel stops determines each player's score.

DID YOU KNOW?

The custom of giving chocolate coins at Christmas was thought to have been started by the man who would become known as Saint Nicholas. Nicholas was the bishop of the village of Myra in Lycia, which is now modern-day Turkey. Although there isn't any written documentation, many legends speak of his kindness. He was said to have been an incredibly shy person and wanted to give money to the poor children of his village without them knowing about it. One night, he climbed onto a roof and threw a purse full of money down a chimney, which landed in a pair of stockings that a little girl had hung up to dry. Every year, Nicholas would give coins or money to the children of Myra.

Much later, different customs would include their own special version of hiding coins around the house for children to find. Over time, the coins eventually became chocolate treats and were put into the stockings of children on Christmas morning.

Childhood Memories

Chocolate coins figure in many people's fond childhood memories, such as discovering that your stash had melted in your pocket, or that unforgettable moment when you first inadvertently chewed the aluminum foil. Ripping the mesh bags made us feel like the Incredible Hulk—we may not have realized that the chocolate was waxy, but we didn't really care. Getting into them with our chewed-off kid fingernails sometimes proved challenging, but we were up to the task. The braver ones just popped the whole coin in their mouths and bent it in half, causing the coin to break free from its golden prison.

TWELVE MONTHS IN THE PURSUIT OF CHOCOLATE

For the avid chocolate fan, there are so many events, museums and destinations around the world that one could cater to his or her chocolate obsession by gallivanting the entire globe and doing something different every month of the year. And just to be different, let's start backwards.

December: Chocolate Cruise

The age-old adage that it isn't the destination but the journey that matters rings especially true for passengers on the Chocolate Cruise. Setting sail from Fort Lauderdale, Florida, to the Caribbean, the cruise features baking classes given by master chefs, chocolate tastings and seminars—all of which may make travelers want to castaway and stay on the boat.

November: Haute Couture Fashion Show

Those who swear that chocolate makes their clothes shrink will love the New York Chocolate Show. November is Chocolate Month in New York, and since 1997, the Big Apple has been the annual host to some big chocolate. A chocolate-themed fashion show has runway models strutting wearable clothes made from the good stuff. Dark, white and milk chocolate, chocolate chips and chocolate squares all make an apperance on chocolate dresses, lingerie, shirts and tops. Chocolate purses, earrings, handbags and, of course, shoes also all serve as sweet and fragrant feasts for the senses.

For those unable to make the fashion show, all the haute couture dresses and accessories are put on display for the rest of the festival. The New York Chocolate Show has a little something for everyone—chocolate tastings, demonstrations, shopping, cookbook launches and author signings are just a small part of the festivities. There is also an art show and a Chocolate Lounge, where jolly and over-sampled festival-goers can test various chocolate liqueurs.

Chocolat: Un, Haute Couture: Zéro
If designing chocolate clothing sounds like a dream job, experts say that working with chocolate is much tougher than eating it.

The chocolate itself must be kept at a very low temperature, and the ambient air must also be kept cool. Chocolate fashions are not only the ultimate test of chocolate-making, but also sewing and fashion design knowledge.

Which begs the question: Who makes the chocolate fashions—chocolatiers or designers? The answer is both. This collaborative effort has collections designed by some of the leaders in the fashion industry and executed by chocolatiers and pastry chefs. Hailed as a showcase of creativity, the show requires designers and chefs to express themselves according to a particular theme.

October: Paris Fashion Show

All of the fun of the New York Chocolate Show and even more is available in Paris at the famous Salon du Chocolat. Bigger, bolder and even more decadent than the New York festival, chocolate authorities swear that it is the place to be. Every October, this six-day event is host to thousands of curious and hungry onlookers. Attendees are also invited to help choose the winner of the Miss Cocoa Butter title, who, according to the Salon website, should embody the values of chocolate and express a certain "chocolate attitude, a multicultural image of enjoyment."

Paris hosts 130 chocolate makers from around the world and, like its New York twin, parades chocolate clothing. A Choco Dance Exhibit features festivities, dances and songs combined with the Chocolate Awards and a life-sized wall of chocolate graffiti, making one wonder how to find the time to actually eat chocolate. No matter the choice of activity, this happy event makes visiting the City of Lights a little more luminous.

More in October: That's Amore!

For the rest of the month, tool on down to Perugia, Italy, for Eurochocolate. Home to Baci chocolates since 1922, the Italians are serious about their chocolate and celebrate it in all its forms. Perugia may be the best place to try chocolate pasta and gorgonzola chocolate cheese. And stay overnight at the nearby and affordable Chocohotel, which has floors named after different types of chocolate. Anywhere else it might look strange, but here rooms are decorated in different shades of chocolate brown.

September: All Aboard the Chocolate Train!

You might as well make the most of your time in Europe and hop over to Switzerland. You can hardly call yourself a connoisseur and not visit one of the foremost countries in fine chocolate. The Swiss Chocolate Train leaves Montreux on a meandering trip through the Swiss Alps. With great views of Lake Geneva and some unbeatable Sound-of-Music scenery, the landscape will make you want to yodel your way to Gruyères, where you can pick up some hard yellow cheese and visit a castle. Then it's all engines go to the Cailler-Nestlé chocolate factory in Broc.

August: Canada's Chocolate Capital

Next, it's over to Canada for a visit to St. Stephen, New Brunswick, the country's self-proclaimed "Chocolate Capital." The Ganongs are one of Canada's best-known chocolate dynasties and have been in business since 1873. Their claim to fame is creating the first-ever heart-shaped chocolate box. St. Stephen opened a museum in 1999 and is host to a community favorite, the Chocolate Fest, which takes place during the first week of

August. Festivities include a chocolate-themed brunch, a treasure hunt, a musical concert series, a chocolate-pudding-eating contest for the kids and "choctail hour" for the adults. "Chocolate Lover of the Year" is announced, and wildlife can sometimes be spotted when the festival mascot, Chocolate Mousse, roams the town. For the only time all year, the Ganong factory opens its doors for public tours.

July: Eating Chocolate Never Felt So Good

It's the beginning of hurricane season in the Caribbean, and while you may not be thinking about it, the Grenada Chocolate Company is. This co-op was originally created in an attempt to revolutionize the cacao-chocolate system that typically keeps production separate from harvesting, thereby taking advantage of cacao farmers.

Operating on the belief that farmers should benefit as much as manufacturers, the Grenada Chocolate Company works closely with the neighboring plantation. The chocolate-making machines run on solar-generated electricity, the chocolate is fair trade and organic, and the finished product is delivered by sailboat throughout the Caribbean. As if that isn't enough, all profits from special bars named after hurricanes Ivan and Emily go to Hearts and Hands of Grenada, a local hurricane-relief organization.

June: A Pilgrimage to Chocolate Mecca

In the summer months, a visit to "Chocolate Mecca"—Hershey, Pennsylvania—is in order. Visitors can take a guided trolley tour through the town and see the community that Hershey built, while listening to the history of Milton Hershey and his rise to Chocolate Czar. Stopping at Chocolate World, visitors can buy and eat chocolate and go on interactive chocolate rides.

May: Long Grove, Illinois

Believe it or not, Illinois is the place to be on the first weekend of May every year, when Long Grove is transformed into a chocolate paradise. Attendees can eat their way through the entire business district, which is home to over 80 different stores and restaurants. Chocolate pastries, candy, popcorn, desserts, chocolate pasta and chocolate drinks are on offer; expert chocolate chefs are on site to demonstrate their chocolate-making skills; and children are encouraged to participate in an unusual chocolate/candy fashion show.

April: Roald Dahl Museum

Fans of *Charlie and the Chocolate Factory* can head to Great Missenden, England, to visit the Roald Dahl Museum. Author of the well-loved novel, Dahl has donated early drafts of the book and other memorabilia to the museum. The best part is that kids can find out what it feels like to be Willy Wonka when they design and decorate their own chocolate bars.

March: More Museum Mania

In Cologne, Germany, a visit to the Imhoff-Stollwerck Museum is worth the time it will take you to practice pronouncing the name. Visitors can participate in interactive displays and learn what it feels like to be a wild cacao pod in the simulated rainforest. With more than 3000 years of chocolate history housed in a building made almost entirely out of glass and shaped like a ship's bow, the museum may have you as interested in its architecture as in its chocolate displays. Perish the thought!

In Bruges

The Chocolate Museum in Bruges, Belgium, is housed in a building dating from 1480. With an auspicious start first as a tavern and then a wine store, the museum building certainly seems destined to house only good things. Besides detailing the history of chocolate, the museum also highlights why chocolate is so good, why it's good for you, and how it has become so important in Belgium.

February: Take Me Home, Chocolate Roads

You liked Italy so much that you decided to return. February is the month of love, so how could you celebrate with your Valentine anywhere but Turin, the city that is home to the very best chocolates that Italy has to offer? The CioccolaTÒ festival is an annual event in Turin, where you can dance off some of the chocolate you ate while listening to the tunes of budding musical groups and top names from the Italian Cabaret. This festival also features "Chocolate Roads," a tour that takes you through the entire chocolate-making process, from picking the beans to eating the final product.

January: Romantic Winter Wonderland

End (or start) your year with a bang. Guests at the Blantyre resort near Lenox, Massachusetts, can opt for an ice picnic complete with piping hot chocolate, breathtaking mountain vistas and skating waiters. Fresh, homemade batches of hand-cut marshmallows are included as part of the indulgence.

And for Next Year ...

It's been a busy year. Maybe next year you can try visiting these other chocolate festivals:

- **February:** Scottsdale Fine Art and Chocolate Festival in Arizona

- **September:** Ghirardelli Square Chocolate Festival of San Francisco

- **October:** Divine Chocolate Festival in London, England

CHOCOLATE IN UNLIKELY PLACES

Jamaican Hot Chocolate

Believe it or not, Jamaicans drink hot chocolate. At the Royal Plantation in Ocho Rios, guests can sample this masterpiece, which is made from cacao beans that are dried and roasted on site and spiced with grated, locally grown cinnamon.

Cuban *Cacahuatl*

There is a chocolate museum in Havana, though by some accounts, it is less of a museum and more of a café that serves chocolate and has a few posters on the wall. Either way, open since 2003, the museum offers information on the history of cacao and its harvesting, production and commercialization. What it offers that others don't is *cacahuatl*. After the "tour," visitors are invited to taste hot chocolate prepared the traditional way or, for the most extreme adventurers, the Aztec way.

Argentina: Quest for the Oompa-Loompas

Bariloche, in the Patagonia region in South America, is known as the "Aspen of Argentina." But chocolate lovers aren't there for the skiing. After World War II, when European immigrants brought their chocolate-making skills with them to the region, they left a legacy of incredible chocolate delicacies. And it will probably come as no surprise that once a year, this country's top tourist destination hosts a chocolate feast. If you've ever wondered where Loompaland is, you may stumble across it here where, if you're lucky, little men with a huge bowls of melted chocolate will dip cherries and lay them out on a tray for the enjoyment of passersby.

Manila's Chocolate Girls

In the Chocolate Room at the Manila Peninsula Hotel, the people who make the thousands of chocolates needed daily for the hotel are deaf. The hotel has been hiring hearing-impaired employees, fondly referred to as the "Chocolate Girls," for more than 30 years. An integral and capable part of the team, the Chocolate Girls make every piece of chocolate at the Peninsula by hand.

Vietnam: The Sofitel Metropol

If the words "chocolate" and "buffet" can be equated to a symphony of perfection in your ears, you may want to stop by the Sofitel Metropol in Hanoi. With a crepe station, a chocolate fountain, chocolate ice cream, hot chocolate made right at the hotel and a cornucopia of chocolate as far as the eye can see, chocolate aficionados will be floating on a scrumptious cloud of cocoa. With unlimited helpings of mousse, macaroons, brownies, cannelloni, chocolate bread pudding, truffles, bonbons, éclairs and chocolate bombe, the only trouble that fans may have is deciding when to stop.

SUKKULAAT
in Greenlandic

CHOCOLATE FOR LUCK

Japan: "Kitto Katsu"

Initially produced by Rowntree as the Chocolate Crisp, Kit Kat is believed to have taken its name from the famous 1920s club of the same name in London. Kit Kat is a top-seller in England and now belongs to candy giant Nestlé.

Though rice-based sweets are still more popular than chocolate in Japan, Kit Kat's popularity increased when it became a "spokesbar" for good luck in Japan. Pronounced in Japanese as "Kitto Katsu," the name roughly translates as "definitely win," which can be taken to mean "I will succeed" or "I hope you win." Students buy it for good luck before exams. The Japanese are highly superstitious, and mothers in that country give Kit Kats to their children as a sign of encouragement.

Some Japanese don't really see the connection and claim that the name translates only very loosely. Either way, the Nestlé higher-ups must have gotten down on their knees in gratitude for the beauty of linguistic misinterpretation. Or did they?

Happy coincidence or clever ploy by the manufacturer, Bob Campbell, a communications manager and webmaster of alpha-male.com, believes it was a "brilliant, subtle, incredibly patient advertising and public relations campaign." Sponsored by Nestlé, hotels began giving away free Kit Kat bars a few years ago as lucky charms to the students who descend annually on Tokyo by the thousands to write their university entrance exams.

Far-Out Flavors

Not coincidentally, Nestlé launches a new flavor in Japan every year right around exam time. To date, Japan has produced about 45 different versions and flavors of Kit Kat, most of them limited-edition bars exclusive to Japan. Some flavors include peach, apple, strawberry, melon, bitter, cherry, red bean, brandy and orange, lemon cheesecake, passionfruit, custard pudding and, of course, matcha green tea. The most unusual flavor—soybean.

Korea: Putting Chocolate to the Test

In Korea, November 15 is University Entrance Exam Day. Competition is fierce, and high school seniors study for months to prepare for the six-hour exam that will admit them into one of the top three universities. Korean teenagers can spend up to 16 hours a day studying, since their futures depend almost exclusively on the name of the university they attend. Students enrolled in leading universities can expect to be invited by top companies to take lucrative jobs that may very well set them for life.

Before the exams, two-foot-long chocolate axes and forks are given to high school seniors as symbolic gifts to help them "spear" the right answers. Encouraging the students is a countrywide effort—high school bands and cheering crowds of well-wishers meet test-takers at school gates; workers report to their jobs an hour later than usual to reduce rush-hour traffic. Landings and takeoffs at Seoul's Kimpo International Airport are even banned for two 15-minute intervals in the morning and evening so as not to distract students during the listening-comprehension portions of the exam. Even the U.S. military halts training at its 90 bases in South Korea for nine hours out of respect for this tradition.

FOR THE LOVE OF CHOCOLATE

Valentine's Day Superstitions

Some superstitions are better known than others—black cats, broken mirrors and sidewalk cracks are all omens of bad luck— but few realize that there are superstitions and fables associated with Valentine's Day, our national day for love. Single women may want to take notes.

On Valentine's Day, single women going about their morning routine may want to be careful. According to legend, the first man's name she reads in the paper or hears on the TV or radio will be the name of the man she will marry. Let's hope Brad Pitt makes the morning news!

Single women should avoid squirrels, an animal that can sometimes symbolize hoarding. Spotting a squirrel on Valentine's Day means a woman is destined to marry a cheapskate who will hoard all the money.

What a woman should really keep an eye out for are goldfinches, small birds that supposedly carry the good portent that she will marry a millionaire. Seeing a robin on V-Day means you will marry a crime fighter, while strangely, seeing a bat means you will marry a baseball player.

If you find a glove on the road on Valentine's Day, your future beloved will have the other missing glove. Lastly, seeing a flock of doves on Valentine's Day portends a happy, peaceful marriage, which is why some new couples choose to include them in their wedding ceremonies.

Sadly, no mention about gorging oneself on chocolate being a good luck omen, but why chance it? In the meantime, chocolate can substitute as our one true love.

Sweet Dreams

Many people love chocolate so much that they dream about it in their sleep. Just like everything else, chocolate has symbolism associated with it. Generally speaking, food in dreams symbolizes food for new thoughts, ideas or beliefs. Dreams help us digest ideas mentally.

According to the *Dream Dictionary*, the symbolism of a chocolate dream varies depending on what we are doing while eating the chocolate. Are we stealing it from somebody else or sharing it with a friend or lover? If the dream is positive, then the chocolate symbolizes happiness and good health. Chocolate also satisfies and consoles people when they are feeling unhappy.

If you dream of getting a stomachache or toothache from eating chocolate, you need to curb overindulgence in foods of any kind or perhaps search for what is making you feel unhappy.

HALLOWEEN SUPERSTITIONS

Superstitions surrounding Halloween, the biggest chocolate and candy day of the year, abound, though most people don't give them much thought while they are munching away on their sweets.

Trick or Treat

Most Halloween traditions can be linked back to the Celts, particularly the Irish. Some theories say that many of our modern-day Halloween traditions originated from the Celtic festival of Samhain (pronounced *sow-in*), the Celtic new year.

Trick-or-treating originated in Ireland. On Halloween night, wealthy landowners gave food to the poor in the hope that visiting ghosts of the night would see their good deeds and spare them from trouble. The Irish were also said to leave bowls of fruit outside their doors to appease the spirits. Mischievous children dressed like ghosts would then run around pretending to be spirits and steal the fruit.

Another theory proposes that the tradition possibly originated from beggars knocking on doors to ask for food in exchange for prayers for dead family members. Some even say that Druid priests would go door-to-door demanding money for their rituals and torturing those who refused.

The Irish potato famine in the mid-19th century resulted in the migration of some two million Irish to the United States, who brought the tradition with them.

Most modern-day children would surely tell you that they are glad that candy and chocolate have replaced fruit as Halloween-night donations.

Fun Halloween Facts

- Next to Christmas, Halloween is the most celebrated and commercially successful holiday.

- From a marketing perspective, Halloween is the sixth most profitable holiday after Christmas, Mothers' Day, Valentine's Day, Easter and Fathers' Day.

- Chocolate bars are the number-one favorite candy of trick-or-treaters.

- In the U.S. alone, sales of Halloween candy average $1 billion per year.

- Now a popular Halloween treat, the Tootsie Roll was the first "penny candy" to be sold with a wrapper.

- There were a total of 1170 chocolate-producing and/or manufacturing establishments in the U.S. in 2006, employing 39,457 people and shipping $13.9 billion worth of goods. California led the nation in the number of chocolate- and cocoa-manufacturing establishments at 128, followed by Pennsylvania with 116.

Nuts to Satan
Maybe the popularity of chocolate and candy has something to do with an old superstition. The British used to believe that Satan was a nut-gatherer, so on Halloween, nuts were used as magic charms.

CHOCOLATE TALES

Chocolate as Superhero

The Izapan, a people closely associated with the Olmec, treated cacoa as a divine product handed down to human beings from the mythical Mountain of Sustenance. An ancient legend, retold by Carol Off, is a story in which one of the so-called Hero Twins—the children of the male and female deities who created the universe—is decapitated. His head is then posted on a cacao tree, where it manages to impregnate the ruler's daughter, who gives birth to other Hero Twins. These offspring subsequently save humankind from the "evil denizens of the underworld."

So the next time someone tells you that chocolate isn't good for you, you can tell them that it can help save humankind from evil.

Drinking in Church

The following story of chocolate folklore is a well-known one and is presented here as retold by Thomas Gage.

The upper-class white ladies of Chiapa Real in Mexico around 1630 claimed that they felt so weak and nauseous during church services that they couldn't possibly survive an entire sermon without a cup of soothing, revitalizing hot chocolate. It was therefore necessary for their maids to bring them a cup during mass. The bishop of Chiapa was so frustrated by the constant interruptions that he posted a notice stating that food and drink were no longer permitted in the church, and anyone not abiding by these rules would be excommunicated. The women took no notice of the bishop's warning and carried on drinking their hot chocolate. Eventually the situation escalated to where swords were drawn against the priests as they tried to take the cups of chocolate away from the ladies-in-waiting as they brought the drinks to their mistresses.

The furious women slighted the church and began attending mass at the convents instead. The local priest warned the bishop to heed the ladies, who would surely seek revenge if they did not get their way.

Sure enough, the bishop fell ill and died a most unpleasant death eight days later.

Rumor had it that a gentlewoman "noted to be somewhat too familiar with one of the bishop's pages" persuaded the innocent young man to deliver a cup of poisoned chocolate to "him who so rigorously had forbidden chocolate to be drunk in the church." It seemed that, in private, the bishop was a real glutton.

The moral of the story: A man should never get in the way of a woman and her chocolate.

Having the Last Word

Another tale of the dangerous powers of this elixir tells of an 18th-century gentleman who believed himself to be the best preparer of hot chocolate in the region. He was so shamelessly boastful about his abilities that he wounded the pride of a woman who believed that she herself held this precious talent.

Deeply offended, she took her revenge by offering him a cup of poisoned chocolate, which the unfortunate man drank to the last drop. As he felt the first fatal pains, he was still able to make one last judgment: "Your chocolate, dear lady, would have been much better had you used a bit more sugar to hide the poison. Think about this next time."

Poisonous Passion

The Marquis de Sade also enjoyed exploring the deadly aspect of chocolate. In his novel *Juliette*, a sleeping powder is secretly put into the chocolate drink of one character, Menski, to make him sleep, and poison is put in the cups of young Rose and Madame Brissac to get them out of the way as well.

Born to Be Wild

In April 2007, Latvia gifted the small Estonian island of Ruhnu with an 88-pound chocolate bear. This symbolic gift was offered to commemorate the Latvia-to-Estonia voyage made by a live bear the previous year. The 70 residents of Ruhnu were mighty surprised by the visiting bear when it floated into town on a chunk of ice.

The renegade bear eluded capture and lived as a fugitive in the roughly five square miles of forest that cover the island. A summer celebrity, the bear is thought to have voluntarily ended his vacation and gone back to Latvia.

Fortunately, the live bear didn't sample any of the residents of Ruhnu, though the same can't be said for his chocolate counterpart. The chocolate bruin sent to commemorate the odd event that boosted Ruhnu tourism was divided up equally among all 70 of the island's residents and eaten.

Ice Cream for a Cause

In July 2008, Ben & Jerry's launched a new chocolate ice cream to commemorate Elton John's first concert date in Vermont. The chocolate base with peanut butter cookie dough, butter brickle and white chocolate chunks was called "Goodbye Yellow Brickle Road" and paid homage to Elton's famous 1970s hit. Sadly, the ice cream was only available for one week, but all the profits went to benefit the Elton John AIDS Foundation.

SOKOLATA
in Greek

FOOD FIGHTS

Seeing Red

The spring of 1947 saw one of the most peculiar strikes of the 20th century.

After World War II, the price of chocolate bars rose from five to eight cents in Canada, marking an almost 60-percent increase. On April 25, 1947, a small group of angry teen activists in Ladysmith and Chemainus on Vancouver Island, BC, began a chocolate crusade in front of local candy stores with signs reading "Eight Cent Bars—Phooey!" and "Candy's Dandy But 8-Cents Isn't Handy."

Dubbed the "War of the Nickel Bar," the boycott lasted less than two weeks but swept across the country. Children all across Canada took to the streets to protest the outrageous increase in chocolate bar prices. The Ganong brothers had managed to keep their bar at five cents in New Brunswick, and children in other parts of Canada were simply asking for equal treatment.

For the most part, adults had begrudgingly accepted inflation as a by-product of the post-war economy, but the children would have none of it.

The crusade had a ripple effect and started to perturb adults who were fed up with the never-ending price increases on all consumer goods after the end of the war. The children had plenty of backing from the media and even politicians, all of whom resented the rising cost of living.

Besieged manufacturers pointed out the loss of profitable wartime contracts and the increased cost of everything, including cacao beans, sugarcane, packaging and labor, that made the price increase inevitable. They tried unsuccessfully to reason with the protestors, but the children had them by the Jersey Nuts.

Suddenly, the tide turned against the children. A right-wing Toronto publication shamelessly accused them of being unpatriotic and suggested that the protest had communist ties. Parents, school principals, police officers, priests and youth club leaders quickly mobilized to stop what had suddenly been characterized as a threat to national security.

Overnight, the protest had become malicious, and the children were unexpectedly branded as "delinquents threatening civic order." Communist fears ran rampant at the time, and the general public got caught up in Cold War rhetoric, believing that the boycott had roots in Russia, under Stalin's direction. "Chocolate bars and world revolution may seem poles apart but to the devious Communist mind there's a close relationship," wrote the publication.

Although it seems ludicrous now, the article was enough to bring the candy wars to an end once and for all. The children, after two lively weeks of staking their claim in the chocolate universe, were forced to accept that the cost of their beloved chocolate bars would stay at eight cents.

Good Chocolate Makes Good Neighbors

For the longest time, a flower shop was the only business permitted in the vicinity for the privileged residents of Manhattan's Park Avenue. When it was discovered that the flower shop was just a front for a lucrative heroin trade and was shut down, an entrepreneurial Korean businessman tried to step in and start a legitimate business. The unsuspecting immigrant proposed opening an all-night delicatessen, much to the disdain and chagrin of the residents, who felt that such an establishment was beneath their affluent surroundings. A protest group was formed against the "inappropriate" delicatessen because the residents of Park Avenue did not want to look out their windows at vegetables. The shopkeeper did some research and asked the residents what type of establishment they could abide having in their community. He set up a deluxe import store that carried elegant vegetables, expensive coffee and imported chocolate and has heard nary a complaint ever since.

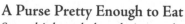

A Purse Pretty Enough to Eat
Some high-end chocolatiers make chocolate handbags that are perfect replicas of the decidedly more expensive, longer-lasting, designer originals. Like their counterparts, these pretty purses are available in a variety of rich combinations and come complete with tiny bows and straps.

Confectionery Christ Going Too Far, Say Some

In March 2007, a controversial chocolate exhibit in New York planned during Easter was canceled after an outcry by Roman Catholics. *My Sweet Lord* was a naked, anatomically correct, chocolate statue of Jesus Christ by Canadian artist Cosimo Cavallaro. The six-foot-high sculpture was created from more than 200 pounds of milk chocolate, with arms outstretched as if on an invisible cross. Cavallaro, whose artistic expression borders on the eccentric, is notorious for a number of quirky food-as-art masterpieces. Previously, the artist had repainted a Manhattan hotel room in melted mozzarella, sprayed five tons of pepper jack cheese on a Wyoming home and decorated a four-poster bed with 312 pounds of processed ham.

DID YOU KNOW?

The world's tallest chocolate sculpture measures about 22 feet tall and is made of 2200 pounds of chocolate. It took chef Alain Roby about 30 hours to build and replicate Rockefeller Center, the Empire State Building and the Chrysler Building.

KOKOLEKA
in Hawaiian

CHOCOLATE-FLAVORED ODDITIES

Invention, my dear friends, is 93 percent perspiration, 6 percent electricity, 4 percent evaporation and 2 percent butterscotch ripple.
–Willy Wonka

Happy Accident

Chocolate is responsible for the microwave—sort of.

Percy Spencer was strolling through a laboratory one day with a chocolate bar in his pocket. He was a scientist working in a post–World War II lab that was trying to create better radar detectors. When he was experimenting with a device called a magnetron, he noticed that the microwaves from the magnetron caused the chocolate in his pocket to melt. This led Spencer to believe that perhaps it could also cook food.

His first endeavor was to try popping corn, which, thank goodness, worked. His next experiment, though successful, left egg on his face—literally. The egg cooked so rapidly that it blew up in his face!

Green Chocolate

Think that chocolate makes the world go round? Well, soon it could make your car go round. It turns out that chocolate waste can be made into fuel. All those deformed, discarded Easter eggs and expired chocolate bars could finally have a home other than the landfill. There are several ways in which this could be done. One way is to have bacteria convert the chocolate into burnable hydrogen gas; the other is to turn it into biodiesel.

Feeding chocolate to *E. coli* bacteria would ferment the chocolate waste and produce hydrogen gas. Still in its initial stages, the research shows great promise. A cheap alternative to fossil fuels, not only would this method reduce waste organically and economically, it would also produce no new waste. In laboratory tests, chocolate produced enough hydrogen to power a fuel cell that ran a small fan. The only waste it created was water.

In December 2007, Andy Pag and John Grimshaw journeyed 4500 miles in a chocolate-powered vehicle. Made from 8818 pounds of chocolate misshapes—the equivalent of 80,000 chocolate bars—the chocolate biodiesel powered them from England to Timbuktu in West Africa. The chocolate-derived ethanol was blended with vegetable oil, and the Britons used 396 gallons to complete their journey. Not only was the expedition carbon neutral, it was carbon negative. Ultimately, they used less carbon on their voyage than they would have if they'd stayed at home. The fuel is made from cocoa butter but, sadly, does not look or smell like chocolate.

How's that for chocientious?

Chococlock

For chocolate lovers with an indulgence-control problem, there is a perfect invention—the Chococlock. Built like a cuckoo clock, it dispenses a chocolate treat once an hour on the hour to the tune of the "Dance of the Sugar Plum Fairy." Perhaps enthusiasts can get their exercise by rushing to retrieve the chocolate within the allotted 30 seconds, after which time a shutter closes, and the candy lover is "shut out" of luck. And forget about leaving your desk to talk to a co-worker—this invention might actually increase productivity by keeping you at your desk...or it may just as easily decrease it by causing you to stare in breathy anticipation as the clock ticks down to the next hour.

Chocoholics who break into a sweat and experience heart palpitations at the thought of eating only one chocolate per hour will be glad to hear that there is a cheat button that will deliver a chocolate whenever the button is pressed. So, really, this is no different than a candy dish, except that it plays Christmas music year round.

Gifting Chocolates in Europe a Potential Land Mine

You have to tread carefully when giving chocolate to someone in Europe. Chocolate signals class and rank, social standing and even nationality. The kind of chocolate you give is a dead giveaway to who you are and what you think of the people to whom you are giving the gift. Chocolate is taken very seriously in Europe. Belgians believe their chocolate is the best in the world, while the French believe their chocolate is also the best in the world, and the Swiss would argue that, no, in fact, theirs is the best.

In Paris, it is not only the type of chocolate you bring, but from which shop in which neighborhood and on which street you buy it that can make or break your social standing. Chocolate can take you on a social journey and open doors. Some even claim that bringing the "right" type of chocolate to a party, gathering or corporate function will improve your standing more than a work permit or residency card.

The Most Expensive Dessert in the World

Chocoholics with $25,000 burning a hole in their pockets can head down to the Serendipity-3 restaurant in New York and buy a really fancy ice cream. The "Frrrozen Haute Chocolate" has been declared by the *Guinness World Book of Records* to be the world's most expensive dessert, though really, it just sounds like a really clever publicity stunt.

The dessert is a take on the restaurant's famous frozen hot chocolate and is a blend of 28 different types of cocoa, including 14 of the most expensive and exotic from around the globe. Mixed with one-fifth of an ounce of 24-carat gold, the chocolate is then topped with whipped cream and…more gold.

No ordinary cherry tops this sundae. Instead, it is garnished with La Madeline au Truffe, which, of course, is the most expensive chocolate in the world. At $250 per truffle, the Madeline contains a rare French Périgord mushroom truffle surrounded by high-quality Calrhona dark chocolate.

People get to eat this expensive dish with a gold spoon decorated with diamonds. At the base of the goblet is an 18-carat gold bracelet set with diamonds. The buyer gets to keep the bracelet and the spoon, which took more than three months to design, and digest the rest. The truffle has to be flown in from France, the gold from Switzerland and the cocoas from around the world, so before you book your flight to New York, don't forget to pre-order the expensive dish two weeks in advance.

In a cruel twist of fate, the restaurant was temporarily closed for three weeks after having failed two health inspections in one month. Various publications and television news reports of mice and cockroach infestations left residents joking about whether there was more than chocolate and edible gold in that $25,000 dessert. If Frrrozen Haute Chocolate is too rich for your blood, the restaurant also offers the world's most expensive pie, which can be purchased for the bargain price of $14,260. As well, the restaurant offers a "Golden Opulence Sundae" for $1000. Requiring advance notice of only 48 hours, there is no word on whether or not you need to share this indulgence with any rodents.

Danger! Radioactive Chocolate!

Once upon a time, responsible mothers everywhere would cover their babies in a thin layer of radium-enriched lotion while coating their own faces with the "radiant" beauty cream and drinking atomic sodas from a straw.

Shortly after its discovery in 1898 by Marie Curie and her husband, Pierre, radium became the new magic potion. In the 1930s, radium-containing products were praised as a cure for almost all conceivable diseases, including arthritis, cancer, blindness, indigestion and fatigue. There was even a radioactive capillary tonic to "aid hair growth." In 1953, a Denver company promoted a radium contraceptive gel to customers. The beauty industry also got on board, promoting face cream, toothpaste and bath salts.

In the same vein, people starting to feel their age may have bought a chocolate bar in the 1930s containing radium and sold for its "rejuvenation power."

People believed that radium was going to save the world, and in the early part of the 20th century, radium-containing products flooded the market. Such products fell out of vogue in many countries after it was discovered they could have serious adverse health effects. Authorities began banning the products when people started dying.

Treat Yourself to Chocolate, Radiation-Free

A luxury retreat in Hakone, Japan, west of Tokyo offers chocolate baths every Valentine's Day. This spa also offers wine, Japanese sake, green tea and coffee baths.

In Hershey, Pennsylvania, the chocolate bath has been around since the new millennium. At Hershey's day spa, indulge in a bath of whipped cocoa or try a Peppermint Patty chocolate treatment, a hydrotherapy treatment or a cocoa massage. Chocolate fondue body wraps are also available—strawberries and fruit not included.

A resort in Germany offers salutary chocolate baths, which are said to moisturize dry skin and leave you smelling fabulous. Meanwhile, a hotel in Bavaria has opened what it claims is Europe's first chocolate spa suite, where guests can enjoy a chocolate-based massage and body wrap. The treatment includes a body peel with dark chocolate flakes, a body coat with hot chocolate sauce and a massage with orange and chocolate-truffle oil. The spa claims that the mineral salts and vitamins contained in cacao beans render the treatment scientifically healthy.

More Chocolate Indulgence

In Geneva, Switzerland, you can get a chocolate body wrap or a chocolate bath with real grated chocolate and cocoa butter. While you are there, pick up a French-English dictionary so you can figure out what the local favorite, *les poubelles de Genève*, translates to. The truffle-like filling of these delicacies makes them taste like anything but garbage.

Dyeing for Chocolate

Chocoholics looking for other unique ways to indulge in chocolate without the calories can now buy T-shirts dyed in melted chocolate. A T-shirt outlet in Honolulu, Hawaii, appropriately named Crazy Shirts, will also dye shirts in Kona coffee, blue Curaçao liqueur, beer, hemp, chili, key lime, money and, randomly…volcanic soil? The scent will fade after several washings, but until then the shirt will leave you smelling like a bar of freshly laundered chocolate.

Craving a Game?

There is a chocolate version of the famous Parker Brothers game of Monopoly. Called Chocolate-opoly, the game takes the bite out of real estate. Wrapped chocolates scrumptiously replace houses and hotels. Chocolate chunks can be traded for chocolate factories, and players may need to pay conching fees or get sent to Chocoholics Anonymous. Playing pieces include a piece of cake, a Valentine's box or a bonbon. Canadian chocolate lovers will be glad to know there is also a Canadian version.

But Chocolate-opoly isn't the only chocolate version of a famous board game. Scrabble, Trivial Pursuit, chess and poker, among others, are also available. The poker version has chocolate "chips" but does include a standard set of playing cards. Chocolate Scrabble comes with chocolate playing tiles, and chocolate chess has pieces crafted out of white and milk chocolate on an edible chocolate playing board. When one player takes the other player's piece, the piece is eaten.

WEAPONS OF MASS DIGESTION

Everything in this room is eatable. In fact, even I am eatable, but that is called cannibalism my dear children and is frowned upon in most civilizations.

–Willy Wonka

Chocolate for Dinner

A collection of recipes created by an Italian priest during the 18th century shows the Italians' long tradition of using chocolate in savory dishes. Among the collection are recipes for fried chocolate-dipped liver, chocolate pudding with veal and candied fruit, chocolate soup and chocolate polenta.

Think we've come a long way since the 18th century? Think again. It's not just the Italians who pair the weird with the wonderful. Other gastronomic grievances have been created all across the United States by modern-day enthusiasts.

DID YOU KNOW?

A Chicago-based company sells mind-boggling combinations such as white chocolate with kalamata olives and dark chocolate with cardamom, walnuts and plums.

Taking It to Extremes

People will take just about anything and either deep-fry it or dip it in chocolate—sometimes both. Creations run the gamut from chocolate-covered Twinkies and fortune cookies to chocolate beet cake, chocolate sushi and, believe it or not, chocolate-covered bacon. All three seemingly inappropriate and unlikely pairings are alive and well and possibly living in your colon.

If the thought of chocolate beet cake makes you squirm, there is a way to make it sound better—just imagine caramelized chocolate onion cake and chocolate sauerkraut cake. See? Chocolate beet cake doesn't sound so bad now, does it? Can chocolate make even spoiled cabbage taste good? Some devotees swear that it can! There are a bevy of new culinary train wrecks that dare to test the Chocolate Lover's Law that just about anything goes well with chocolate. And if you believe that, maybe you are also the perfect candidate to try out chocolate hummus or potato chip brownies.

Bacon Bonbons

Another company testing out the Law is a boutique-confectioner called Vosges Haut-Chocolat, which recently introduced a chocolate bacon bar to the world. Made of 41 percent cocoa, a milk chocolate shell smothers a slab of smoked bacon sprinkled with salt. Since it was introduced, strips of chocolate-dipped bacon have been turning up in store windows and state fairs all across the United States. The confection has also been given the unfortunate moniker of "pig lickers" or "bacon bonbons."

Chocolate Sushi?

Diners in South Korea have the option of ordering chocolate-covered meat floss sushi. Scrambled egg, meat floss, cucumber and chocolate drizzle. Maki, shrimp, wasabi, rice and… chocolate? With soy dip on the side? It's an acquired taste.

If the real thing doesn't do it for you, there is a happy and much more appealing alternative—chocolate shaped to look like sushi. Made with Belgian or Swiss chocolate, this sweeter variety is realistic, hand-rolled and undoubtedly tastier than its savory counterparts. And a bonus—the "soy sauce" is made of chocolate.

Mmm...Crunchy!

If all this culinary mayhem doesn't faze the chocolate lover in you, you may want to try the wide selection of chocolate-covered insects. Grasshoppers, caterpillars, ants or crickets—you can have them straight up or blended with toffee brittle to take the edge off.

Hot Beef Sundae

Chocolate purists need not worry—beef isn't horning in on chocolate. The Hot Beef Sundae debuted at state fairs and carnivals—including the Calgary Stampede—all across the U.S. and Canada. A bowl of hand-mashed buttery potatoes topped with roast beef, cheddar cheese and a ripe cherry tomato, the Hot Beef Sundae isn't really a sundae at all. Chocolate aficionados worldwide are breathing a sigh of relief.

Creepy, Crawly Chocolate!
Bugs are a typical ingredient in chocolate with an average of 80 bug fragments per 100 grams.

CSOKOLÁDÉ
in Hungarian

DRINK UP!

Fancy a Pint?

Finally! Something for beer drinkers and chocolate lovers alike. If *theobroma* (the scientific name for cacao is *Theobroma cacao*) means "food of the gods," then chocolate beer must be the drink of the gods. In the late 1990s, Young's Brewery in London, England, was one of the first to introduce a chocolate-flavored beer, Double Chocolate Stout.

Soon afterwards, Danish brewery giant Carlsberg added chocolate to their mash and released the limited-edition Criollo Stout. Featuring English licorice and dark chocolate and made with six different kinds of malt, this unfiltered beer is said to have contained tiny flecks of chocolate. Since then, many more countries have come up with their own versions and (pardon the pun) "hopped" onto the brew wagon.

Made with bittersweet Dutch chocolate, Rogue Chocolate Stout from Rogue Ales in Oregon was originally brewed for export to Japan as Chocolate Bear Beer. It is stronger and drier than Young's stout. Belgian-owned Brewery Ommegang in Cooperstown, New York, produces the Chocolate Indulgence, which lives up to its name. Japanese beer maker Kirin makes a premium chocolate beer slated to hit shelves in December 2008, and Sweden has a chocolate stout made by a small brewery in Bredaryd. In the U.S., Brooklyn Brewery and Samuel Adams also have their own delicious versions of chocolate "brewfection."

This trend is trying to target a broader demographic, with breweries hoping that chocolate beer will appeal to women, who are typically not big beer drinkers.

Homer Simpson Has Died and Gone to Heaven

Shenandoah Brewing in Alexandria, Virginia, makes Chocolate Doughnut Beer, an oatmeal stout that reportedly tastes like a sugary Krispy Kreme doughnut.

Sweet Pairings

All this may leave you wondering: What does one eat with chocolate beer? Well, definitely not chocolate, which would make the pairing too sweet. Some recommendations include serving a nice, pungent blue cheese with the Rogue Chocolate Stout or serving a fruity dessert such as a blueberry tart or cherry cobbler with the Chocolate Indulgence.

Frozen Beer on a Stick

The latest craze to hit Virginia is frozen beer on a stick, created by a chef when he unintentionally froze his cherry-flavored beer and realized what a delicious mistake he had made! The new summertime favorite, appropriately named "Hopsickles," is available in a variety of flavors, including chocolate stout.

Other wacky beer concoctions include chocolate beer milkshakes, beer ice cream and, for the extremely adventurous, chocolate beer floats. Use any chocolate-flavored beer, add a few scoops of chocolate ice cream and some chocolate shavings and—*voilà!*—a new taste sensation.

Súkkulaði
in Icelandic

Alcoholic Chocolate Drinks

There are many different types of alcoholic chocolate drinks, from decadent chocolate-flavored liqueurs to smooth chocolate vodkas. With their sweet cocoa aromas, these drinks are delicious on their own or mixed in your favorite coffee, "choctail" or recipe. For "grown-up" versions of their favorite recipes, some chefs like to use chocolate liqueurs as a substitute where chocolate syrup or extract is called for in the recipes.

Chocolate Liqueurs

Chocolate liqueurs contain natural and/or artificial chocolate flavoring with a brandy or neutral spirit base. Sometimes cream is added for a smooth, creamy texture. From there, flavorings such as mint, chocolate, coconut, hazelnuts or coffee may also be added.

There are many well-regarded brands of chocolate liqueurs from a variety of countries. A chocolate hedonist could spend years building a repertoire by gathering liqueurs from all over the world—Mexico, Spain, France, Switzerland, New Zealand and even Latvia all have national brands. Here are a few to get you started:

- **Godiva**: One of the favorite and best known of the North American brands, the chocolate base of this liqueur is of good quality and comes in white, milk, dark or cappuccino.

- **Mozart:** This Austrian company creates its liqueur in all the usual flavors—milk, white and dark chocolate—but also has an Amadé ChocOrange flavor. A mix of dark chocolate with blood oranges, this intriguing variation would taste great on ice cream.

- **Afrikoko**: This Tanzanian product made with chocolate from West Africa and Canadian grain alcohol has coconut for all you imbibers hoping to bring a tropical feel to a cold winter's night.

- **Ashanti Gold and Vermeer Dutch Chocolate Cream**: These both hail from the Netherlands and are worth sampling.

- **French Royal**: Say *bonjour* to chocolate liqueurs in a dizzying array of banana, cherry, coconut, French coffee, mint, nut and orange flavors.

- **Conticream**: This Australian liqueur combines whisky, coffee and chocolate together, which, by the sounds of it, will have you "down under" the table after only a few shots.

- **Bottega Gianduia Chocolate Cream**: This Italian liqueur is an infusion of chocolate and grappa that could give the Bicern de Gianduiotto a run for its

QUIRKY, LITTLE-KNOWN AND DOWNRIGHT WEIRD FACTS

money. This liquid dessert has been equated to a chocolate fondue from a shot glass with a kick at the end. There is so much chocolate in this drink that the bottle requires a good shake so the liqueur doesn't come out lumpy.

Hemel op Aarde: With a name that translates as "Heaven on Earth," chocophiles might want to try this Dutch liqueur made of distilled cherries, cherry blossoms, almonds, chocolate, rum and various types of honey and sugar. This sugar grenade may make your dentist happy, but who are we to resist?

Other liqueurs you may want to try include Cheri Suisse, a sweet, cherry-chocolate-flavored liqueur from Switzerland, and everyone is raving about Tiramisu chocolate liqueur, which is great in cakes and truffles. Other brands include Alchemy and Sxul, Lejay Lagoute, Monin, as well as Polmos Lubushka from Poland and Xanath from Mexico. Try them if not for the quality, then for the name. There are no testimonials as to quality or taste from this author, but feel free to conduct your own field tests.

Crème de Cacao

Crème de cacao is similar to chocolate liqueur, only not quite as sweet or syrupy. This liqueur is flavored with cacao or vanilla beans and is usually available as "dark" or "brown." The alcohol content ranges from 15 to 25 percent, which equates to 40 to 50 proof, making it divine in chocolate martinis—the white variety is often used in a Grasshopper and the brown in a Brandy Alexander.

As with chocolate liqueur, there is an equally wide range of crème de cacao on the market, both imported and domestic. Some brands include Marie Brizard, Hiram Walker, Bols, Arrow, Jacquin's, McGinnis, Meaghers Dark and De Kuyper.

Cocktail Hour

The Brandy Alexander, as its name indicates, is the brandy version of the gin-based Alexander cocktail. To make it, you need the following:

1 oz cream
1 oz dark crème de cacao
1 oz brandy
ground nutmeg for garnish

Pour the ingredients into a cocktail shaker with ice cubes. Shake well, then strain into a chilled cocktail glass. Garnish with a dusting of nutmeg. Repeat.

The Grasshopper is a great dessert cocktail. To make it, you need the following:

3/4 oz cream
3/4 oz white crème de cacao
3/4 oz green crème de menthe

Pour the ingredients into a cocktail shaker with ice cubes. Shake well, then strain into a chilled cocktail glass. Repeat.

Schnapps

Some of you are probably cringing at the word "schnapps," which likely conjures up remnants of foggy memories of raiding your parents' liquor cabinet and imbibing the sweet, syrupy mixture—and living to rue the results. Schnapps, along with some other alcohols such as tequila, has the dubious reputation of being the most revolting drink ever tasted, mostly because of uninformed overindulgence during our teenage years when we didn't know any better.

The thing about schnapps is that it isn't meant to be drunk straight up. Use a good-quality product wisely and sparingly, and the results will be quite different than if you use a poor-quality substitute.

Schnapps contains the same base as chocolate liqueurs but is loaded with sugar, and sugar equals hangover. Schnapps should be used sparingly and not as the main ingredient in a drink or recipe.

Schnapps is a German word meaning "liquor." I always thought it meant schnapp your fingers and you'll be sick.

Schnappy Suggestions

Here are a few suggestions for schnapps liqueur that might just change your opinion of this drink forever:

- **Teichenne (Spain):** This entirely natural-flavored schnapps comes from a family-owned distillery in the Catalan region of Spain. Natural ingredients and real fruit essences are combined to make schnapps in a variety of flavors, including chocolate, vanilla, peach, apple, butterscotch, melon, lemon, strawberry, raspberry, banana, green apple, kiwi, blackcurrant, coffee and coconut. Call it alchemy or call it indecisiveness, but it looks as if they robbed all the fruit off Carmen Miranda's hat for this drink.

- **Godfrey Chocolate Spice Schnapps (Mexico):** Inspired by an Aztec recipe, this schnapps blends the taste of chocolate with a hint of spiciness to add a kick to the flavor.

 DID YOU KNOW?

Berentzen in Germany is one of the best-known producers of schnapps.

Scandalous Schnapps

Right before Valentine's Day, a junior high school in Iowa had to pull an edition of the student newspaper off the shelves because it contained a hot chocolate recipe that included peppermint schnapps.

A student at the West Des Moines school submitted the recipe. The school's principal said that the recipe slipped through the editing process, but that the student who submitted it had made an honest mistake—the student thought that schnapps was a type of candy.

Chocolate Vodka

Perhaps not quite as scandalous, but surprising all the same, chocolate vodka tastes better than you might expect. Here are a few of the most popular chocolate varieties:

- **Goldenbarr**: This import from Ukraine claims to be the world's first chocolate vodka. Goldenbarr is an 80-proof vodka that uses pure cacao bean extract, meaning that the taste is a little stronger and less sweet than some of the other 70-proof chocolate vodkas.

- **Kerenski**: Like the Russians, this vodka is uncomplicated, not fussy and packs quite a punch. Use it to make a Chocolate Russian by combining one part chocolate vodka, two parts Kahlua and five parts chocolate milk. Shake. Drink. Repeat.

- **Iganoff**: This Polish vodka is triple-distilled for purity and then infused with cocoa.

Ultimat: Poland's most expensive premium vodka is sold in hand-blown crystal bottles. The chocolate-vanilla version is said to go well in coffee or hot chocolate.

Czekoladowa: This is a premium distilled Polish grain vodka infused with an authentic melt-in-your-mouth chocolate taste.

Kremlovskya Belgian Chocolate Vodka: The Belgians know chocolate as well as the Eastern Europeans know vodka, and this is their entry in the vodka category.

Three Olives: The British may not be the foremost authorities on vodka or chocolate, but they sure know how to drink. This premium vodka made in England is smooth, but its 35-percent alcohol content will mean the necessity of appointing a designated driver.

Vodka Chocolates

If chocolate vodka doesn't interest you, it is also possible to buy vodka-infused, ganache-filled chocolates. A British brand, Elizabeth Shaw, sells these potent pods in tubes of four packages, each one containing a different flavored vodka chocolate: neat, orange, vanilla and raspberry. The chocolates are also available in tequila and schnapps flavors.

BIZARRE AMERICAN FOOD HOLIDAYS

Can Lima Bean Respect Day Be Any Match for National Chocolate Mousse Day?

In the United States, there is a food holiday for almost every day of the year. Some are much more understandable than others. You may not see the point of having a National Fluffernutter Day on October 8 or think that Moldy Cheese Day on October 9 is worth observing, but everyone can surely understand the importance of National Ice Cream Day (July 21).

The president of the United States approves these events or days. Petitions are drawn up by interested parties and introduced to the Senate. Sometimes state or civic governments will proclaim these special days, which is why there can be a National Chocolate Month, as well as two National Chocolate Days, authorized at different levels of government. Every one of these holidays has a sponsor—a person or group that has spent money to convince Congress and/or calendar makers to include the holiday. Either way, this is a win-win for the chocolate diva in all of us.

So, if National Submarine-Hoagy-Hero-Grinder Day on October 9 isn't up your alley, maybe some of the following chocolate-themed observances will be.

January: National Candy Month

January 3: Chocolate-Filled Cherry Day

January 10: Bittersweet Chocolate Day

January 22: National Blonde Brownie Day

January 27: Chocolate Cake Day

February: National Celebration of Chocolate Month

Is it any surprise that February was chosen as National Celebration of Chocolate month? What may surprise you is that in the past, February was considered a slow month in snack-food sales. So it is now National Snack Food Month and National Potato Lover's Month. Not coincidentally, these observances are sponsored by the Snack Food Association and the National Potato Promotion Board.

If all that junk food proves to be too much for you, fear not—February is also Fiber Focus Month and National Grapefruit Month.

Other important dates not to be missed in February include:

February 2: Heavenly Hash Day and Crepe Day (in France)

February 5: National Chocolate Fondue Day

February 6: Nutella Day

February 11: Peppermint Patty Day

February 14: National Creme-Filled Chocolates Day

February 19: National Chocolate Mint Day

February 25: National Chocolate-Covered Nuts Day

February 28: National Chocolate Soufflé Day

February also shares stranger, less popular food holidays such as Crab-Stuffed Flounder Day (February 18), Molasses Bar Day (February 8), Don't Cry Over Spilled Milk Day (February 11) and the ever-popular Dog Biscuit Appreciation Day (February 23).

March: National Nutrition Month

You'd never know that March is National Nutrition Month! The second week in March is Chocolate Chip Cookie Week, while the third is American Chocolate Week.

March 6: National White Chocolate Cheesecake Day

March 8: National Peanut Cluster Day

March 19: National Chocolate Caramel Day

March 24: National Chocolate-Covered Raisins Day

March 28: Something on a Stick Day—if you are desperately craving chocolate, surely you can scrounge up something to make this day about chocolate

It's not chocolate related, but just so you know, March 30 is Turkey Neck Soup Day.

April: National Food Month

Opportunities to eat chocolate abound in April, with National Bake Week beginning on the first Monday of the month.

April 3: National Chocolate Mousse Day

April 21: Chocolate-Covered Cashew Truffle Day

April 23: National Cherry Cheesecake Day

Not to be missed this month—Lima Bean Respect Day
(April 20)

May: National Chocolate Custard Month

Special days this month include:

May 1: National Chocolate Parfait Day

May 2: National Truffles Day

May 5: National Chocolate Custard Day

May 6: International No Diet Day—though not specifically
chocolate themed, surely some chocolate could be eaten

May 9: National Butterscotch Brownie Day

May 11: Eat What You Want Day (chocolate!)

May 12: National Nutty Fudge Day.

May 15: National Chocolate Chip Day

May 19: National Devil's Food Cake Day

June: National Candy Month and National Dairy Month

June 2: National Rocky Road Ice Cream Day

June 7: National Chocolate Ice Cream Day

June 11: National German Chocolate Cake Day

June 16: National Fudge Day

June 22: National Chocolate Éclair Day

June 26: National Chocolate Pudding Day

July: National Ice Cream Month

The third Sunday of the month is Sundae Sunday.

July 3: National Chocolate Wafer Day and Eat Beans Day—what a combo!

July 8: National Chocolate with Almonds Day

July 21: National Ice Cream Day

July 22: National Penuche Fudge Day

July 25: National Hot Fudge Sundae Day

July 28: National Milk Chocolate Day

August...

If you managed to plow your way through all that ice cream in July, look out! August is National Brownies at Brunch Month.

August 20: National Chocolate Pecan Pie Day

And, hopefully, National Pots de Crème Day on August 27 won't interfere with More Herbs, Less Salt Day on August 29.

September: National Cholesterol Education Month

September 12: National Chocolate Milkshake Day

September 22: National Ice Cream Cone Day

September 23: National White Chocolate Day

September 27: National Chocolate Milk Day and, luckily, National Corned Beef Hash Day

October...

Although October has been slated as Eat Better, Eat Healthier Month, it has also been designated National Dessert Month, National Cookie Month, National Pizza Festival Month, National Caramel Month and, of course, Eat Country Ham Month, so eating better and healthier might prove tough.

October 1: Homemade Cookies Day

October 7: Bittersweet Chocolate with Almonds Day

October 14: National Chocolate-Covered Insects Day
(Do chocolate-covered insects really need their own day? One thing is for sure, food holidays are equal opportunity—no one gets missed here.)

October 18: National Chocolate Cupcake Day

October 28: National Chocolate Day

November: National Peanut Butter Month

November 8: National Harvey Wallbanger Day

November 9: Cook Something Bold and Pungent Day (garlic chocolate, perhaps?)

November 26: National Cake Day

November 29: Chocolates Day

November 30: National Mousse Day

December: National Fruit Cake and National Eggnog Month

This brings us to the last and most decadent month of the year, though if you have been following these dates and eating accordingly, you might have to declare a National Exercise Day.

December 4: National Cookie Day

December 8: National Chocolate Brownie Day

December 12: National Cocoa Day

And because it is the last month of the year, and to make sure all our bases are covered, you can celebrate National Chocolate-Covered Anything Day on December 16.

And if you aren't completely stuffed from National Pumpkin Pie Day on December 25 or National Candy Cane Day on December 26, then by all means, celebrate National Chocolate Candy Day on December 28.

DID YOU KNOW?

You don't even need government approval to proclaim your own day. If you have enough money to promote the event, go right ahead! The American government doesn't even have a trademark on the word "National," so there is no law saying your day has to be declared by Congress.

REALLY HOT CHOCOLATE

Self-discipline implies some unpleasant things to me, including staying away from chocolate and keeping my hands out of women's pants.

–Oleg Kiselev

The Magic of Chocolate

Chocolate has long been praised as a potion for love, bringing relief to the broken-hearted and causing lusty stirrings in the nether regions of both men and women.

Love Potion No. 9

Aztec emperor Montezuma was said to have been a dedicated drinker of hot chocolate—up to 20 cups a day—believing that it fuelled his lovemaking and made him virile. To that end, he drank a gobletful each time he entered his harem. Maybe he was onto something. Italian researchers have found that women who eat chocolate are more amorous and reach orgasm easier than those who do not indulge.

An Aristocrat's Viagra

French kings loved their mistresses as much as French women loved their cups of chocolate. Madame du Barry, mistress of Louis XV, is believed to have offered the sybaritic liquid to all her suitors before they were invited into her bedchamber.

Legendary lover Casanova is reported to have preferred chocolate to champagne as an inducement to romance.

Is It True What They Say About the Green Ones?
The urban legend about the aphrodisiac effect of eating green M&Ms is part of a long tradition of ascribing amorous powers to chocolate. Mars Inc. says the company has no idea how the rumor started.

Marquis Marq and the Funky Bunch

The Marquis de Sade was a notorious French writer and a rogue who had no qualms about putting pen to paper about his exploits. Chocolate was an ingredient in the well-known aphrodisiac Spanish fly. In the following tale, the Marquis de Sade colorfully describes a typical evening out:

> "Into the dessert he slipped chocolate pastilles so good that a number of people devoured them…but he had mixed in some Spanish fly…those who ate the pastilles began to burn with unchaste ardor.… Even the most respectable of women were unable to resist the uterine rage that stirred within them. And so it was that M. de Sade enjoyed the flavors of his sister-in-law."

The Real Thing

In the George Orwell classic, *1984*, characters Winston Smith and Julia live in a totalitarian society where chocolate is "dull, brown crumbly stuff that tasted…like the smoke of a rubbish fire" and sexual enjoyment is prohibited by the state. Julia gives Winston a piece of real chocolate, "dark and shiny…delightful," just before they defy the law by whole-heartedly making love.

After about twenty years of marriage, I'm finally starting to scratch
the surface of [what women want]. And I think the answer lies
somewhere between conversation and chocolate.

–Mel Gibson

DID YOU  KNOW?

The Italians have their own version of the Hershey Kiss.
Perugia's classic Baci chocolates have been exchanged as gifts by
lovers since they were first introduced in 1922. *Baci* means
"kisses" in Italian, and each chocolate has a romantic message
hidden beneath the foil wrapper.

Bad to the Bar

In Switzerland, the Zurich Council banned chocolate in 1722.
Chocolate had a reputation as an aphrodisiac, and concerned
citizens were afraid that chocolate could be put to improper
uses, such as seducing women.

Literary Love

Chocolate has elicited numerous poems, sonnets and movies
and has been mentioned in many books.

A James Wadsworth quatrain:

A Curious History of the Nature and Quality of
Chocolate

'Twill make Old women Young and Fresh;
Create New Motions of the Flesh,
And cause them long for you know what,
If they but taste of chocolate.

Sex in the Souk

A very conservative country, Syria masks a lesser-known side—a sexuality that is never publicly expressed. Beneath the black clothes and in the privacy of homes, the evidence of different lifestyles are evident in the very risqué lingerie shops in the souk marketplaces. These shops, run by men, carry an enormous assortment of transparent women's underwear in bikini form, sporting feathers, fur, ribbons and lace. Some break into bird-song or Arabic music when touched.

The pièce de résistance is a chocolate ensemble in which everything can be licked off but the straps. Storeowners say they don't sell to Western countries. Their clients are Syrians and Saudis as well as women from the Emirate countries. The new vogue in these countries, apparently, is the use of remote control, rented video cameras to record the many changes of elaborate wedding gowns worn by brides on their wedding night.

What use are cartridges in battle? I always carry chocolate instead.
–George Bernard Shaw

Like Water for Chocolate

In many Latin American countries, hot chocolate is made with water instead of milk. The expression "Like water for chocolate" is translated from Spanish and refers to the boiling temperature of water needed to melt chocolate. Metaphorically, the phrase refers to someone who is angry and has reached his or her boiling point, like water ready to be used to make hot chocolate.

Mexican author Laura Esquivel used the expression in her popular 1989 novel of the same name as a metaphor for passion and sexual arousal. The 1993 movie based on the novel became the highest grossing foreign film ever released in the United States at that time. Hip-hop rapper Common also used the title for his fourth studio album.

Serendipity
Esquivel's latest novel, *Malinche* (2006), explores the life of a near-mythic figure in Mexican history—the woman who served as Spanish conquistador Hernan Cortés' interpreter and mistress. The novel speaks to Mexico's long and rich connection with chocolate.

> *Oh, divine chocolate!*
> *They grind thee kneeling,*
> *Beat thee with hands praying*
> *And drink thee with eyes to Heaven.*
> –Marco Antonio Orellana (18th century)

Pregnancy Cravings

During pregnancy, women often have cravings for unusual food combinations. A survey has suggested that pregnancy cravings are much more common among modern women than in previous generations. More than 75 percent of pregnant women have cravings, compared to just 30 percent 50 years ago. Milla Jovovich admitted to craving bone marrow during her pregnancy and spent an entire day searching the streets of Paris to find some. Even more bizarre, about 30 percent of pregnant women also experience non-food-related cravings for things such as coal, soap, toothpaste, sponges, mud, chalk, matches, rubber and laundry soap! This indicates a condition known as pica, which is often more a matter of smell and texture, rather than taste.

Chocolate cravings are a little less unusual during pregnancy. Pregnant or not, craving chocolate is pretty normal, especially for women.

Celebrity Cravings

Naturally, celebrities get cravings, too. Angelina Jolie was so desperate for Reese's Pieces while she was pregnant with twins in Namibia that she called the Hershey factory in Pennsylvania and had an entire crate shipped directly to her in Africa. The chocolate-and-peanut-butter treats were unavailable where she lived, and the craving was just too powerful to be ignored.

Jennifer Lopez craved salsa, M&Ms and orange soda when she was pregnant, while Christina Aguilera carbed out on cupcakes, cookies and muffins. For Jenny McCarthy, it was brownies all the way, while Heidi Klum needed ice cream to tame the beast.

KOKLAT
in Indonesian and Malay

CHOCOLATE AND HEALTH

The cocoa bean is a phenomenon, for nowhere else has Nature concentrated such a wealth of valuable nourishment into so small a space.
—Alexander von Humboldt, German scientist

The Magic Potion

Chocolate was originally considered a medicinal product or drug and was popular in royal courts throughout Europe. In the 1700s, chocolate was prescribed by some French doctors as a cure-all for everything from colds to cholera. They prescribed it to help thin patients gain weight, to stimulate digestion and elimination and as remedy for chest infections, diarrhea, dysentery and lifeless libidos. Today, researchers are unearthing all sorts of miracles hidden in this scrumptious, modern-day panacea. With all this good news concerning chocolate, it is no surprise that chocolate consumption is rising three times as fast as the population is growing in the United States.

DID YOU  KNOW?

Many scientific studies on the health benefits of chocolate are funded by chocolate companies.

Walking on Sunshine

Researchers are now starting to support what most of us have known for ages—chocolate makes us feel good.

Phenylethylamine, or PEA, is a substance that is released naturally in the human body when we are in love, and it is believed to be a sexual stimulant. Scientists are now also beginning to explore the positive effects of using chocolate as an antidepressant.

PEA is one of the many components found in chocolate, and low levels of it in the body may cause some common forms of depression. As an alternative to mainstream antidepressants, which prevent the body's own PEA from breaking down, some patients could get the dosage they need from eating dark chocolate. Understandably, this treatment is preferred by some patients as a delicious, all-natural alternative that works when some standard treatments typically have not.

Addictive Substance

Is it possible to become addicted to chocolate? Well, yes, but researchers say that chocolate is not habit-forming. While they agree that it improves mood and increases energy, chocolate does not produce tolerance. Fortunately—or unfortunately, depending on your proclivity—this means that you will not need more chocolate the next time you eat it to get the same effect.

Chocolate is Mother Nature's best-kept secret. We still haven't unlocked all of its mysteries, and reproducing it is out of the question.
–Maurice Jeffery, manufacturing consultant

Eighth Wonder of the World?

To this day, chemists have been unable to synthesize the taste of chocolate, despite decades of research. It is so complex that reproducing it is nearly impossible. Why? Because chocolate contains more than 1200 different chemical components, none of which are dominant, so finding the right combination is very difficult. For example, one chocolate chemical, trimethylamine, emanates a strong odor of spoiled fish that overpowers every other chemical in a test tube. However, real chocolate would just not taste the same without it.

Only 20 percent of the chemicals that occur naturally in chocolate have been approved by the American government for use in foods. For example, scientists have discovered that chocolate contains a cyanide-based chemical.

DID YOU KNOW?

A chocolate bar contains more calcium, protein and vitamin B2 than a banana or an orange.

Lonely Hearts

On your own this Valentine's Day? That's okay, because there are so many reasons why good-quality chocolate is better than a date:

- Chocolate contains theobromine and theophylline, which are gentler, non-addictive stimulants than caffeine. These substances take more time to break down into caffeine and will therefore give you energy and increase alertness and concentration without making you feel jittery.

- Chocolate also contains other stimulants, dopamine and serotonin, that act as pain relievers and mood enhancers.

- Cacao is rich in anandamine, known as the "bliss molecule" because it locks onto cannabin receptors—the active substance in cannabis—creating mild euphoria.

- Chocolate contains trace amounts of phenylethylamine, which is known as the "love drug," and is a substance that is also present in hashish and morphine.

- Chocolate is good for the heart.

- If you invite chocolate over for dinner, it brings its own dessert.

Wild Thing, You Make My Heart Sing

Heart-healthy antioxidants found in red wine, green tea and grape seeds are some of the same as those found in dark chocolate. The darker the chocolate, the more antioxidants it contains. Two ounces of dark chocolate with a minimum of 60 to 70 percent cocoa eaten each day will improve circulation, help blood vessels expand and lower blood cholesterol levels. This decreases the risk of heart attacks, strokes, cancer and heart disease.

Researchers have discovered that chocolate produces some of the same reactions in the brain as marijuana. The researchers also discovered other similarities between the two, but can't remember what they are.

–Matt Lauer, NBC's *Today Show*

DID YOU KNOW?

Hershey Foods Corp. used to extract theobromine from discarded cacao bean shells and sell it to Coca-Cola and other soft-drink manufacturers for use as a stimulant in their products. This lasted until the 1950s, when Coke found cheaper substitutes.

According to a British study in 2004, scientists found that theobromine is nearly one-third more effective than codeine at stopping persistent coughs because it relaxes the smooth muscles of the bronchial tubes in the lungs and has nearly no side effects. Today, traditional Mexican healers, *curanderos*, still commonly prescribe chocolate for bronchitis.

Chocolate for PMS

Ever wonder why women crave chocolate so much when it's that time of the month? Well, it's not all in our heads. Cacao is the plant world's most concentrated source of dietary magnesium, a trace mineral that can help alleviate PMS symptoms. Low magnesium levels produce cravings for the good stuff.

Preventing Anemia

Chocolate also contains copper, an important co-factor in preventing anemia and ensuring that iron can effectively transport oxygen throughout the body.

DID YOU KNOW?

Chocolate helps prevent premature labor and convulsions in pregnant women.

Chocoholics Have Sticky Fingers Crossed

The FBI has profilers who study criminals' behavior to try to find a pattern that will help them capture the bad guys. If your only crime is eating too much chocolate, then metabolic profiling may "capture" your attention.

The next time you sink your teeth into a slab of chocolate, you might feel a lot less guilty about overindulging. It may be beyond your control. A recent study by scientists at the Nestlé Research Centre in Switzerland says there may be a correlation between our metabolisms and our love of chocolate. Chemical signatures, which may be programmed into our metabolisms, are linked with dietary preferences—in this case chocolate—and are measurable by common laboratory tests.

For some, it may come as no surprise that there is a chocolate-loving metabolic type, or metabotype. The chocolate lovers in this study had healthier levels of LDL or "bad" cholesterol than those who could not pass chocolate up. Essentially, the study concluded that if you have a favorable metabotype for chocolate, then you can more or less eat as much chocolate as you want, and it will not affect your LDL cholesterol levels.

People may eventually be categorized by metabotype, which can be used to design a healthier diet, customized to each individual's needs, preferences and reactions to foods. Until then, chocolate lovers are going to have to get by the old-fashioned way—moderation.

Darkly Good
Dark chocolate contains four times the antioxidants of green tea and six times what is found in blueberries.

Not for Everyone

As delicious, healthy and satisfying as it is for humans, cocoa products may be toxic or lethal to dogs and some other domestic animals that aren't able to metabolize theobromine as effectively as humans. A 3.5-ounce dark chocolate bar with a high cocoa content can poison a small dog.

Chocolate can be equally harmful for small forest animals such as monkeys, but there are some that use cacao in other fascinating ways. For example, a woodpecker will make a hole in a cacao pod to attract flying insects that lay their eggs in the sweet inner pulp surrounding the seeds. The woodpecker then returns at regular intervals to eat the larvae.

Leafcutter ants love cacao leaves and carry them to their anthills. Then they wait for fungus to grow on the leaves and eat the fungus.

La Cioccolata
in Italian

THE DARK SIDE OF CHOCOLATE

Chocolate Gets a Bad Wrap

Chocolate often gets blamed for any number of ills and conditions, including migraines, obesity, acne and tooth decay. But the truth is, the culprit is far more likely to be overindulgence or the excess sugar, vegetable fat and added preservatives present in poor-quality, mass-produced chocolate.

Tooth Decay

The cocoa butter in chocolate actually prevents sugar from sticking to teeth. Chocolate contains tannins that counteract the enzyme that causes cavities. It also contains calcium and fluoride, both of which strengthen teeth and fight cavities.

Acne

Poor diet and hormonal imbalances are more likely the cause of this unfortunate condition. Furthermore, because cocoa butter stays liquid at normal body temperature, it will not clog arteries, and the body will not have to metabolize the fat as it would have to for the hydrogenated fats found in low-grade chocolate.

In fact, cocoa butter is the perfect emollient for the skin and is more effective than the petroleum jelly used in some cheap body-care products. It is also used in the manufacture of a small percentage of cosmetics.

Pure Bliss

What do chocolate cravings, forgetful mice and blissful pigs have in common? The answer is anandamine, a molecule that plays a role in pain, depression, appetite, memory and fertility. The name comes from *ananda*, the Sanskrit word for "bliss," and is a compound present in chocolate.

BITS AND BITES

Mousse or Mayo?

When chocolate mousse was first invented, it was known as chocolate mayonnaise.

Fake Blood

The "blood" used in the shower scene of the thriller movie *Psycho* was actually chocolate syrup. Janet Leigh's famous scene took over seven days to shoot.

Dessert with a Sting

Archipelago, a restaurant in London, England, is known for its exotic specialties. One of the dessert options is a chocolate-covered scorpion with a sip of sweet white wine.

Eating in School

"Chocolate school" is an annual two-week seminar at the University of Wisconsin, where industry workers learn the science behind chocolate and candy manufacturing.

Chocolate Helps Your Memory

Eleanor Roosevelt ate three chocolate-covered garlic balls each morning as a memory aid. She doesn't remember any of it.

Watch What You Eat

Chocolate truffles are so called because they resemble the highly prized fungus of the same name.

Cross-Border Chocolate

Canada is the top exporter of chocolate to the U.S.

So That's Where It Comes From!

The Ivory Coast produces 40 percent of the world's cocoa beans.

Hot Cocoa

Cacao is grown almost exclusively within 20 degrees of the equator.

The First Chocolate Cake

The world's first recipe for a cake made with chocolate was created by the Austrians in 1778.

Astronaut Food

Every Russian and American space voyage has included chocolate bars.

SHOKORA, CHOKORE-TO
in Japanese

CRAZY FOR CACAO

Cacao Tree Facts

The scientific name for the cacao tree is *Theobroma cacao*. *Theobroma* means "food of the gods."

Flowers and fruit occur simultaneously on the tree.

The tree produces about six to nine pounds of beans per year and yields a crop twice a year.

Forastero, Criollo and Trinitario are the three main varieties of cacao beans that are commercially cultivated. The Criollo are widely considered to be of the best quality.

The flowers of the cacao plant are pollinated by midges. Midges are small, winged insects that make their home in rotting leaves on the forest floor.

Cacao Coat of Arms

Two countries in the world feature cacao on their national coats of arms:

In Fiji, the national design bears a shield with an image of a lion holding a cacao pod across the top of a red St. George's cross. This shield is also featured on Fiji's national flag.

The coat of arms of Ghana consists of a shield divided into four quarters by a green St. George's cross. The bottom-left quarter displays a cacao tree, which represents the agricultural wealth of the country.

DID YOU  KNOW?

Research is being carried out into other uses for cacao such as fertilizer, animal feed and jams.

Doing It the Traditional Way

The *metate* is a primitive, hand-operated mill used by the Mayans as an all-purpose mixer to turn cacao beans into a paste. It is still used today in Belize to make '*kuh-kuh* and in Mexico to make traditional hot chocolate.

ŠOKOLĀDE
in Latvian

CHOCOLATE JOKES

Make a Wish

A man found a bottle on the beach. He opened it and out popped a genie, who gave the man three wishes. The man wished for a million dollars and—*poof!*—there was a million dollars. Then he wished for a convertible and—*poof!*—there was a convertible. Then he wished to be irresistible to all women and—*poof!*—he turned into a box of chocolates.

Better Than Sex

For the serious chocoholic, chocolate is better than sex. If you believe that, you *really* need to meet that special someone who will change your mind. If you have *already* met that special someone and still believe that, I *really need* to know where you get your chocolate!

Dying for Chocolate

An elderly man lay dying in his bed. In death's agony, he suddenly smelled the aroma of his favorite chocolate chip cookies wafting up the stairs. Gathering his remaining strength, he lifted himself from the bed. He slowly made his way out of the bedroom and, with even greater effort, forced himself down the stairs, gripping the railing with both hands. With labored breath, he leaned against the door, gazing into the kitchen.

Were it not for death's agony, he would have thought himself already in heaven. There, spread out on the kitchen table, were hundreds of his favorite chocolate chip cookies. Mustering one final effort, he threw himself towards the table. His aged and withered hand was painstakingly making its way towards a cookie when it was suddenly smacked by a spatula.

"Stay out of those," said his wife, "they're for the funeral."

Short and Sweet

Q: What do cannibals eat for dessert?
A: Chocolate-covered Aunts.

Working for Peanuts

An old man and a young man worked in offices next to each other. The young man noticed that the older man always had a jar of peanuts on his desk. The young man loved peanuts.

One day, while the older man was away from his desk, the young man could no longer resist and ate over half the peanuts in the old man's jar. When the old man returned, the young man felt guilty and confessed to taking the peanuts.

The old man responded, "That's okay. Since I lost my teeth, all I can do is lick the chocolate off the M&Ms."

Making Fun of Everyone

The following jokes work equally as well for a variety of different crowds. Substitute the word "blonde," "redneck," "hippie," "your boss" or the name of any other demographic you wish to insult for the word "man" in the jokes below.

Q: How do you know when a man has been making chocolate chip cookies?
A: You find M&M shells all over the kitchen floor.

Q: Why do men hate M&Ms?
A: They're too hard to peel.

Q: What job function does a man have in an M&M factory?
A: Proofreading.

Q: How do you confuse a man?
A: Ask him to alphabetize a bag of M&Ms.

Q: Why did the man get fired from the M&M factory?
A: He threw out the *W*s.

THE ECONOMICS OF CHOCOLATE

Chocolate Consumption on the Rise

According to Statistics Canada, Canadians purchased 14.7 pounds of chocolate per person in 2007. That is up from 2005, when Canadians only purchased 8.58 pounds per capita. In the U.S., sales for 2006 were estimated at close to $16 billion. Chocolate sales are forecast to grow to $18 billion by 2011, according to the U.S. Market for Chocolate. Strong consumer interest in the reported health benefits of dark chocolate and online ordering are believed to partially account for the increased sales.

German Chocoholics

With consumption up 7.8 percent in only three years, Germans now hold the dubious honor of being the world's top chocolate gobblers. They edged out the Swiss, who used to be first and whose consumption has more or less remained the same. Neither Canada nor the United States even ranks in the top 10 of chocolate-consuming countries. However, the average American consumes more than 25 pounds of candy per year, and adults actually consume more than children.

Šokoladas
in Lithuanian

Eating Their Way to the Top

Here's a list of the top 15 chocolate-consuming countries in 2005 and their consumption in pounds per person:

Germany	24.50 (up 7.8% since 2002)
Belgium	24.25 (up 24.2%)
Switzerland	23.60 (down 1.7%)
United Kingdom	22.50 (up 2%)
Austria	20.70 (up 18.35)
Norway	18.70 (up 3.1%)
Denmark	17.02 (down 16.3%)
France	14.90 (down 2.6%)
Finland	14.89 (up 3.7%)
Sweden	14.87 (down 17.1%)
United States	12.27 (up 4.1%)
Australia	11.68 (up 22.1%)
Italy	9.37 (up 8.1%)
Canada	8.58 (no change)
Poland	8.07 (up 11.2%)

What's in a Number?

There is a lot of conflicting information about chocolate consumption. American chocolate companies use 1.5 billion pounds of milk every year and consume almost half of the world's almonds and 20 percent of the world's peanuts, yet they rank 11th on the world scale. Why is this?

The statistics do not account for online purchases or for any products other than pure chocolate. More than 90 percent of Americans consume chocolate in some form every day. To get to that figure, you have to include every item that contains cocoa or a cocoa product: chocolate, chocolate candy, chocolate drinks, chocolate cereals, chocolate ice creams, cookies, cakes, brownies, puddings or any other of the thousands of chocolate-containing products on the American market. All these chocolate items skew the statistics and make this figure seem artificially high.

The U.S. produces more chocolate than any other country. Americans eat an average of 22 pounds of chocolate each year, or approximately 2.8 *billion* pounds annually, split almost equally between candy and chocolate. That is far less than most Europeans consume.

The American palate prefers milk chocolate, approximately 92 percent, but the popularity of dark chocolate is growing rapidly.

Chocolate by Any Other Name

For economic reasons, some candy companies now substitute cheap vegetable oils for cocoa butter in their chocolate bars. This makes the bars waxy and less flavorful. Consequently, chocolate companies are no longer allowed to label them "chocolate bars" if they do not contain cocoa butter, which gives chocolate its smooth, creamy texture. Consumers with a keen eye will notice that some of their favorite and most popular candy brands say they are "made with chocolate" or are "chocolate candy" or have "chocolate coating."

A PART OF OUR LIVES

Making Learning Taste Good

In Canada, teachers have the option of implementing a unit on chocolate. Not in Health class, but in Social Studies. The Global Education Network, the Canadian International Development Agency (CIDA) and the Government of Canada have developed a module for grades 6 to 10 entitled "Chocolate: A Fair Trade and Human Rights Unit," with curriculum links for teachers in Ontario.

British Office Workers Tell All

BBC News reported that security was not a priority for British office workers after a survey revealed that three-fourths of commuters questioned on their way home from work were more than willing to share login and password information with the researchers—in exchange for some chocolate.

National Preferences

According to American writer Nika Standen Hazelton, it is important for manufacturers to know their market. Confectioners would have a hard time selling chocolate in blue wrappers in Shanghai or Hong Kong, for example, because the Chinese associate blue with death. The Swiss and Germans, on the other hand, prefer to have pictures of the product on their packaging.

Know Where to Shop
You can often find excellent products from the best chocolate makers in airports. All they are missing is the ambiance of the chocolateries.

CHOCOLATE SOLDIERS

What Does Chocolate Have to Do with Soldiers, Anyway?

There are a lot of different things competing for the "chocolate soldier" moniker, and just like its sweet namesake, there is a little something for everyone.

The term "chocolate soldier" is an expression first used in World War II to describe new recruits joining the war because it was believed they would melt like chocolate in battle. Since then, the phrase has taken on many different meanings. It can denote a soldier who wilts in the sun or has been conscripted. It can also stand for a clumsy or cowardly soldier or describe one who doesn't know how to fight. Shortened to "chocko" or "choc," this largely pejorative term has come to connote a soldier without heroism or bravery.

The original expression came from a George Bernard Shaw play written in 1894. *Arms and the Man* was later turned into an operetta entitled *The Chocolate Soldier*. The plot is the story of a soldier who prefers to use chocolate instead of bullets in battle. Many versions of *The Chocolate Soldier* were created for film dating as early as 1915 through to 1955.

Chocolate Plants

Can't get enough chocolate? There are also two different species of chocolate soldier plants. The first, *Aquilegia viridiflora*, is known as the columbine form of the chocolate soldier plant and doesn't camouflage as well as a soldier in the jungle, but it is a fighter. This hardy perennial looks almost good enough to eat with its white/dark chocolate appearance. Even sweet to the smell, it blooms in early spring and summer and will help you to enjoy chocolate without preventing you from getting into that bikini.

Chocolate Soldier Pussy Ears

Officially know as the Southern Madagascar shrublet, the *Kalanchoe tomentosa* is also known as the chocolate soldier. These little plants are terrific for those of us who only remember to feed our cats but every other day, as they don't require much attention. In fact, they thrive if ignored. This type of chocolate soldier is brown all around the edges and grows a bit faster than the columbine form.

And Along Came a Butterfly

The chocolate soldier butterfly from Sri Lanka gets its name from its distinctive chocolate brown color. Once the leaves of trees fall, this butterfly fits right in, branded as it is with Mother Nature's own special camouflage. However, it rarely employs this technique, being proud to show off its chocolate color in all its glory. A true brave chocolate soldier.

Wink, Wink, Yoo-Hoo, Chocolate Soldier

From the 1920s through to the 1960s, Chocolate Soldier was a popular chocolate soda drink sold in a glass bottle imprinted with a soldier. It was said to taste very similar to today's Yoo-Hoo chocolate drink. A real sugar grenade, only grittier, this soldier might help you run through the jungle.

Chocolate Soldier Martini

If plays, plants, butterflies and chocolate drinks don't interest you, have no fear—the Chocolate Soldier is also an alcoholic beverage. To make one, combine gin, vermouth and the juice of half a lime, shake it all up and pour the mixture into a martini glass. Now there's something to share with the platoon.

Cikkolata
in Maltese

CHOCOLATE QUOTES

All I really need is love, but a little chocolate now and then doesn't hurt.

–Lucy van Pelt, *Peanuts*, by Charles M. Schulz

Let's just celebrate our agreement with the adding of chocolate to milk.

–Homer Simpson

Life is like a box of chocolates; you never know what you're gonna get.

–Forrest Gump

Venice is like eating an entire box of chocolate liqueurs in one go.

–Truman Capote

I got to thinking about relationships and partial lobotomies. Two seemingly different ideas that might just be perfect together—like chocolate and peanut butter.

–Carrie Bradshaw, *Sex & the City*

Exercise is a dirty word. Every time I hear it, I wash my mouth out with chocolate.

–*Peanuts* by Charles M. Schulz

Strength is the capacity to break a chocolate bar into four pieces with your bare hands. And then eat just one of the pieces.

–Judith Viorst, author, journalist and psychoanalysis researcher

What you see before you, my friend, is the result of a lifetime of chocolate.

–Katharine Hepburn, actress

There's nothing better than a good friend, except a good friend with chocolate.

–Linda Grayson, American author and illustrator

Just as bees will swarm about to protect their nest, so will I "swarm about" to protect my nest of chocolate eggs.

–Jack Handey, "Deep Thoughts," *Saturday Night Live*

Las cosas claras y el chocolate espeso. (Ideas should be clear and chocolate thick.)

–Spanish proverb

After eating chocolate, you feel God-like, as though you can conquer enemies, lead armies, entice lovers.

–Emily Luchetti, pastry chef

The 12-Step Chocoholics Program: Never be more than 12 steps from chocolate!

–Terry Moore, actress

Remember: Patience, discipline, chocolate.

–Unknown

TOP 12 CHEESY ONE-LINERS

- The reason some people eat chocolate is that they don't know what else to do with it.

- Chocolate is by far the most popular of all the many remedies that absolutely won't cure depression.

- I once had an hourglass figure, but the sands of time have shifted.

- Among life's mysteries is how a two-pound box of chocolate can make a woman gain five pounds.

- The average person eats 10 pounds of chocolate a year. Of course, a lot of it goes to waist.

- Eat a square meal a day—a box of chocolate.

- After a bar of chocolate, one can forgive anybody, even one's relatives.

- Man cannot live by chocolate alone—but woman can.

- Nobody knows the truffles I've seen!

- Put "Eat chocolate" at the top of your list of things to do today, that way at least you'll get one thing done.

- Coffee, chocolate, men…some things are just better rich.

- I love a man with chocolate on his breath.

NOT ALWAYS A SWEET BUSINESS

Chocolate and Organized Crime

If the words "organized crime" conjure up images of overweight Italians and money laundering, think again. Organized crime can exist in many different ways and may put some major chocolate manufacturers behind "bars."

Canadian Chocolate "Cartels"

An investigation was launched in November 2007 into allegations that the Canadian divisions of Nestlé, Cadbury, Hershey, Mars and others engaged in a price-fixing scheme in the multibillion-dollar chocolate bar business. According to the Confectionery Manufacturers Association of Canada, Canadians buy about $2.3 billion worth of chocolate and candy every year.

Clandestine Meetings, Whispered Secrets

Search warrants were granted because there are reasonable grounds to believe that these chocolate suppliers created an alliance to try to control the market. According to affidavits, top executives at Hershey, Mars and Nestlé met secretly in coffee shops and restaurants and at conventions to set prices. The Canadian public is protected from these kinds of business practices, which are known as cartels, through the Competition Act.

The companies could face criminal conspiracy charges, which carry penalties of up to $10 million Canadian and/or five years in prison.

Padding Prices

Canada isn't the only country being investigated for pricing shenanigans. In February 2008, the German Federal Cartel Office raided the offices of seven leading chocolate companies, including Mars, Kraft and Nestlé, searching for documents. The German Cartel Office said it suspected that the companies had conspired with one another to raise their prices higher than necessary. Although the increase in the price of raw materials such as cocoa and nuts may have required a slight increase, the companies took advantage of the situation and exaggerated prices even more than necessary. If the office finds evidence of collaboration, the companies face possible fines of up to 10 percent of their annual income.

Because the cost of a chocolate bar is so minimal, most people don't really care about corporate alliances. Most consumers are also aware that this is going on. Oil and gas and diamond prices are fixed, so why should chocolate be different?

Lawsuits in the U.S.

In the United States, it's more of the same. At least 45 similar suits have been filed in eight states on behalf of more than 50 consumer groups and companies. In 2007, chocolate manufacturers' sales in the United States grew by 2.9 percent to $16.3 billion, according to the National Confectioners' Association.

The probe into suspicious business practices came three days before Valentine's Day, one of the peak holidays for chocolate sales. American retail sales of the sweets are expected to exceed $323 million per week, according to Nielsen estimates.

Like Taking Candy From a Baby

Companies looking for a new way to publicize a major event can now say it with candy.

Mars Inc., the maker of M&Ms, is unveiling a new plan called "My Branding," which will allow businesses to purchase large amounts of M&Ms printed with their corporate logo or advertising slogans. Mars already offers a candy branding line called "My M&Ms," targeted at people looking to say "I love you" or "It's a boy" in smaller quantities. And really, nothing says "I love you" quite like an M&M.

Not to be outdone, the Hershey Company has eaten into Mars' idea with Kissables, a candy-coated, kiss-shaped chocolate. They, too, offer a branding option that allows folks to come up with specific messages to be printed on those little flags that stick out of the signature silver wrapping.

For those who might think this is a ludicrous idea being taken too far, the numbers tell a different story. A company spokesperson says the "My M&Ms" line currently generates "between 800 and 1000 orders a day from a database of about 250,000 customers." That doesn't include the ready-made, message-bearing M&Ms that are already in retail stores.

Chocolate is big business and, unlike the founders of some of these companies who let the products speak for themselves and never advertised, marketers these days will brand anything, even if it melts in your mouth.

THE IMPORTANCE OF FAIR TRADE AND ORGANIC PRACTICES

In the Beginning

The Aztecs believed that chocolate was a divine a gift from the Toltec King, Quetzalcoatl, the God of Air, who brought the seeds of the cacao tree from the Garden of Life and gave them to humans. They believed it was Quetzalcoatl's mission to teach mortals how to cultivate various crops. This is a long way from where we are today, now that scientists are trying to genetically engineer chocolate in response to the global crisis.

The Cacao Genome Project

A huge shortfall is being predicted in upcoming years as cacao demand is far outweighing its supply. With cacao crops being affected by fungus, insects and drought, scientists are working on coding the DNA sequences of cacao in an attempt to "safeguard" the world's chocolate supply.

The goal of the five-year project started in the summer of 2008 is to find disease-resistant strains of the plant and improve resistance to drought, which will generally improve crop yields.

Buying Organic

Buying organic has gained popularity in recent years. Food injected with hormones, artificial sweeteners and fats, among other things, has led to an epidemic of childhood obesity in North America and has been linked to cancer, heart disease and many other health conditions. Our relationship with our food has taken a backseat to our ability to spend less at the grocery store. This has caused some consumers to make efforts to eat more consciously and choose quality over price. Craig Sams, the founder of Green & Black's, has supported organic farming for more than 40 years. He is currently chair of The Soil Association, Britain's pioneering organic food and farming not-for-profit organization. He is considered an authority on fair-trade, organic practices. In a 2004 speech given at the IFGene conference in Switzerland, he explained why the solution to today's cacao crisis will not be found at the bottom of a test tube. Portions of his explanations have been reprinted with his gracious permission.

Theory of Evolution

Sams says that Charles Darwin believed that evolution was just a series of mass extinctions punctuated with lucky genetic accidents. A much-lesser-known theory from French biologist Jean-Baptiste Lamarck proposed a different theory of evolution—that an organism can consciously evolve. Crick and Watson, who discovered the molecular structure of DNA in 1953, as well as scientists involved in the Human Genome Project support this theory that acquired characteristics can be transmitted to future generations. For example, there are some who believe that one day, humans will no longer have wisdom teeth—that we have outgrown their need, and by systematically yanking them out for a couple of thousand years or so, eventually they'll get the hint and stop appearing.

The Mayans believed in a similar theory, though of course, it was never articulated as such and expressed itself in a completely different way. What is really fascinating about the Mayans is that they managed to get the cacao tree to evolve simply by respecting and revering its place on Earth.

Sams explains that the Mayans believed in a sort of co-evolution with animals, plants, soil and water. They believed that humankind is characterized by a quest for perfection and that this perfection cannot be achieved without the collaboration of perfected plants and animals. They believed that all organisms on Earth played equally significant roles in the evolutionary process and were valued not solely based on what they could give to humanity, but also, like household pets, loved for themselves and treated with the same care that one would give to a family member. In other words, the Mayans gave back as much as they took from the Earth. And they approached horticulture as a mutual relationship that wasn't just about how much they could get out of any given organism.

The Sacrament of Cocoa

Those that describe eating chocolate as a "religious experience" may not be surprised that the Mayans used cacao together with morning glory seeds as a sacrament to "develop a deeper connection and understanding with plants." If that sounds a little too "far out" for modern-day realists, consider this—it was women who domesticated cacao and created maize. The Criollo bean, which is the cacao industry's most commercially important plant, is a natural deviation of the wild cacao tree and, in the nurturing hands of Mayan women, evolved in ways that are beyond the ability of modern-day plant breeders and molecular biologists to comprehend.

Mayan Women Nurture a Hybrid

The Mayan women, whom Sams refers to as "matriarchal horticulturalists," domesticated the cacao plant and could effect precise changes in developing the Criollo variety while making only minor changes to the original wild plant.

Criollo cacao, which produces the "cream of the crop" seeds, differs from wild cacao in three main ways:

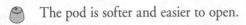 The pod is softer and easier to open.

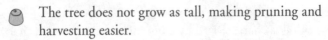 The tree does not grow as tall, making pruning and harvesting easier.

The seeds are purple in the Criollo variety, which reflects a greatly increased content of alkaloids and other compounds. These alkaloids have natural health benefits for humans.

An archaeological expedition to ruins in a remote region of Belize that has not been inhabited since the ninth century made a remarkable discovery—a stand of several hundred domesticated cacao trees that have reproduced without human support on that spot for over a millennium. This is an example of how successfully the Mayans domesticated the cacao plant without depriving it of its intrinsic ability to live in the wild.

Mayans understood what many large conglomerate chocolate manufacturers still haven't gotten—mass-producing cocoa does not work. Developing hybrids to yield more cacao seeds has worked in the short term, but forcing nature to do something unnatural will eventually backfire.

Natural Environment

To understand some of the problems currently being encountered in the Ivory Coast and Ghana, you first have to understand cacao's relationship with its natural environment, and the difference between growing methods, aptly explained by Craig Sams:

> "Cocoa plays an important role in the rainforest where it grows, acting as a link between the canopy, the middle storey and the ground level. The Ancient Mayans knew this and is part of the reason it was so highly respected. Cacao is a unique tree with a unique way of capturing nutrients, protecting itself and reproducing in a harsh environment and rearing its offspring in a caring and nurturing way. It should hardly be surprising then that in the process, it produces substances that have a profound attraction to humans.

In the wild, the cacao tree grows to a height of 10 to 20 metres, which for other trees in the rainforest would mean an inability to survive. To flourish in the middle storey of the rainforest requires a very different strategy. The cacao tree still needs some sunlight, it just gets by with a lot less than most plants need to survive, by exhibiting a frugality and intelligence of function that enables it to live and reproduce in extremely deprived conditions. It tends to do best on hillsides, where glancing light increases the otherwise sparse availability of sunshine. Hence its success in the Maya Mountains, where south-facing mountain slopes allow light to cut through the canopy at an angle."

The Maya were also experts at getting the most use from their land. The trees that provided shade for the cacao also provided them with thatching and building material, fodder, oilseeds, wood, medicines, fruit and allspice.

Different Ways of Farming

Nowadays, smallholder cacao is increasingly shade grown, bird friendly, sustainable and organic. By contrast, plantation-grown cacao constantly has problems with poor management, grower inexperience, slavery, corruption and unreliability.

A well-managed, organic plantation has the following characteristics:

- The plants are grown under shady conditions and are surrounded by a high biodiversity.

- The plants are very fertile, but fertility is delivered over a longer time frame.

- Cultivated cacao takes longer to grow, but the trees last on average 75 to 100 years, instead of 30 years or less.

- The natural wild environment of the cacao tree is replicated.

- The cacao is not as prone to fungal diseases because birds and mammals deposit small amounts of guano and manure onto the leaves of the cacao trees. This is then washed down to the soil by rain. Because the cacao tree is drip-fed natural fertilizer in continuous small quantities, the soft, sappy growth that is prone to fungal and insect attack does not occur.

Compare these now to the most modern and intensive cacao planting methods:

- The trees are closely planted at eight feet apart.

- The trees are grown on cleared land in full sun.

- Fertility comes from regular applications of nitrogen fertilizer.

- Yields are double the "natural" system, but there is no other income from the land. Higher yield means the soil quickly becomes degraded, and farmers must move on and clear-cut more rainforest once the soil is exhausted.

- Disease is rampant and requires constant control. The fungal diseases witches' broom and black pod are common and devastating and are becoming more virulent.

- Overgrowth because of too much fertilizer and sunshine leads to fungal disease in the cacao trees.

This method of farming is left over from a system imposed by American, British, Dutch, German and Swiss "aid" organizations in the 1980s. This massive aid program successfully created global overcapacity in cacao and was a response to the upswing in prices caused by the decision of the Ivory Coast president to hold back supplies from the market in 1982.

Cacao Crash

A conference was held in Costa Rica 1998 at which the leading chocolate companies met to seek solutions to the crash in cacao production. The conference concluded that a return to less intensive practices was the key to sustainable production. However, according to Sams, the legacy of the 1980s aid program will haunt the industry for decades.

Sams explains that it takes one foreman to oversee about four laborers. The reliability of the laborers (and sometimes the foreman as well) is often dubious, and if the trees are planted too far apart, then it becomes increasingly difficult to manage the laborers. Good management depends on lines of sight and voice commands, so planting the trees closer together, though not ideal for the trees, is better for the workforce. The truth is, though, that planting trees more closely creates more problems than it solves.

Also, low world prices and increasing input costs put pressure on labor costs. This leads to increasing dependence on slave labor. This occurs in the Ivory Coast, where slaves are non-Ivorian Africans, and in Malaysia, where tribal people are used. Many of these are women, who are short enough to get under the trees with backpack sprayers to fog the trees with fungicides.

Mother Nature Still Does It Best

Buying organic chocolate honors the relationship between humans and the planet. Continued abuse of the land and attempts to get as much as we can from the cacao tree have and will continue to boomerang—cacao plants in the Ivory Coast and Ghana are suffering from witches' broom, and there are plantations in Brazil where cacao production has collapsed completely.

So with the threat of chocolate extinction, scientists are working to try to genetically engineer chocolate so that the dependence on Mother Nature will be eliminated.

FAIR-TRADE CACAO

Understanding Fair Trade

"Fair trade" and "organic" are two terms that often go hand in hand. Understanding how cacao is grown is only one half of the equation; the rest is realizing what happens to cacao once it has been harvested.

Everyone has likely heard of fair-trade coffee, but may not know that fair-trade cacao is equally necessary. Small-scale farmers are often left out of the bargaining process, and rapidly fluctuating prices can fall so low that the farmers bear the brunt of the losses and are often left without resources.

Belize: The TCGA Cooperative

Buying chocolate picked from the birthplace of cacao is worth its weight in "Maya Gold." Although it may not carry the same cachet as Swiss or Belgian chocolate, rest assured, it is well on its way.

The Toledo Cacao Growers Association (TCGA), a cooperative of 126 members in the southernmost district of Belize, was formed in 1986. Toledo is the poorest district in the country and also has the largest population of Mayan people (both Ketchi and Mopan). Though cacao production is comparatively low compared to the major players in Ghana and the Ivory Coast, it is still very important for the TCGA's producers because it is their main source of income.

The cooperative was formed to allow farmers to demand higher prices, improve their living conditions and help them increase the quality of their cacao. The cacao is grown organically and under a canopy of shade trees that include valuable mahogany, cedar and teak, using sustainable, pesticide-free methods.

Hershey Swoops In

In the mid-1980s, American companies were looking for cacao sources closer to home. The Hershey Chocolate Company set up a Belize-based enterprise and promised to purchase all the cocoa produced in Belize. But they had to adhere to some strict policies and do everything that Hershey demanded of them.

Every farmer would have to spend at least three days at Hummingbird Hershey being trained in the new farming methods and have to offer their land and all their assets as collateral for loans. They had to use a specific Hershey hybrid cacao stock and expensive chemicals at their own cost. The Belizean farmers therefore had to borrow a lot of money to turn their land into productive cacao farms, but were assured that it would be well worth it.

After great effort and much drama, the harvest was finally ready in the early 1990s, and farmers were hugely in debt. When it came time for Hershey to make good on its promises, there was a marketwide price collapse. The original price guaranteed by Hershey was $1.70 per pound. This eventually kept dropping until 1993, when Hershey would not pay more than $0.55 per pound. Essentially, the price for cacao fell so low that it was below the cost of production and the cacao was not worth harvesting. Many farmers were forced to abandon their crops, leaving to search for work elsewhere. The Maya lost land and savings, and the TCGA went bankrupt in 1993.

Fortunately, a chocolate company from the United Kingdom called Green & Black's offered a long-term contract for a stable supply of quality cacao. They agreed to buy all the cacao TCGA could produce at an above-market price. The cacao was used to create Maya Gold Chocolate, the first British fair-trade product, which was introduced in March 1994. Recently, Maya Gold has been enjoying modest recognition as a first-rate chocolate.

Bringing Benefits

More importantly, the contract has turned everything around and helped the cacao growers of southern Belize and their families.

- High school enrolment has increased from 10 percent of the community's children to between 70 and 90 percent.

- A coalition led by the Cacao Growers' Association successfully saved 100,000 hectares of rainforest when they challenged a logging permit granted to a Malaysian company.

- Women's rights and health have benefited. Although the men do the planting, pruning and harvesting, the women control the post-harvest fermentation and drying and therefore control the end product and income from it. Profits have been invested in education, clothing and health.

There are still many challenges to face. Some homes in the region are still without electricity, while others still have only thatched roofs and dirt floors, offering little protection from inclement weather. Crops are often damaged by hurricanes, and more worrisome still, the TCGA may not be able to keep up with the growing demand for organic chocolate.

On top of all that, and unlike some cooperatives in places such as Grenada, where local farmers and producers work together, the Maya will never do more than grow the beans that others make into chocolate. As Carol Off, author of *Bitter Chocolate*, explains it: "Tariff barriers in Europe prohibit finished products from entering the country. Only raw materials are imported, ensuring that consumers get the products they want, and European workers get the manufacturing jobs they need. Until that changes and the Maya can export more than just their beans, they will never be wealthy enough to buy the expensive chocolate bar that bears their name."

Cacao Growers' Festival

Spiced cacao may be nothing new in the Toledo district of southern Belize, going back hundreds of years to the time of the ancient Mayans, but something that is new is the Cacao Festival in Punta Gorda. Only in its third year, it celebrates what some consumers have known for a while—Belizean chocolate is the next big thing.

The festival treats visitors to a full day of Mayan culture and leads them down the Cacao Trail. Activities include visiting organic cacao orchards, meeting the chocolate farmers and enjoying a traditional Mayan lunch before heading to Lubaantun for a special performance of the Deer Dance.

Kukuh, a cacao drink traditionally flavored with ground black pepper, chili and spices and sweetened with forest honey, was consumed hot or cold by the Maya to give them strength. For an authentic cultural experience, watch it being made and sample the bitter brew.

The Deer Dance

The historic Mayan ruins site of Lubaantun is the perfect place to watch the Deer Dance. The dance itself lasts several days, but festival goers are treated to excerpts. Today, the cacao tree is still highly respected by the Maya and is an integral part of their creation myths because they believe that humanity was created out of part of the tree. The Deer Dance evokes the entire history of the Maya and symbolizes the important relationship between humanity and nature.

The Spirit of Cacao

The cocoa tree still holds a great deal of reverence for the Maya. Craig Sams, the man behind Green & Black's, tells a story about witnessing the cutting of a tree that was to be used in the Deer Dance: "It took nearly an hour of explanation, persuasion and extracting of permission from the spirits of the forest and of the specific tree before any Maya would dare to presume to touch it with an axe."

NEW DIRECTIONS

Asia's Untapped Market

European chocolatiers are embracing Asian flavors to sell more chocolate. I will never forget a trip to Korea when I stopped in a local grocery store to pick up an ice cream. It was the season of *Ong Tal Sam*, which in Korean means "hottest part of the summer." Being a teacher, it was the only time I could visit, and it was so hot that even the locals were sweating. Driven by the heat and humidity, I desperately wanted a mango ice cream, which had been my afternoon staple for the last several days, but there weren't any left. I grabbed what I thought was a mint chocolate ice cream bar and desperately started slurping at it before it melted away. Rather than tasting like mint, though, it tasted like dishwater. I had inadvertently chosen a green tea ice cream with red bean filling.

Being only one of many hot, sweaty, white teachers visiting Korea in the hottest part of the summer, my ignorance revealed what most people there already knew—green tea and red bean are big in Asia. In fact, they are some of the most popular flavors.

To Each His (or Her) Own

With European and American chocolate markets at their peak, big-name chocolate producers from both regions are looking to expand in both China and India, where chocolate is not a big seller. As such, manufacturers are experimenting not only with flavors such as red bean and green tea, but also with other flavors such as ginseng and dates. Ginseng is believed to boost energy, relieve stress, fight cancer, regulate blood glucose levels, reduce the risk of obesity and improve sexual performance. In Taiwan and Thailand, an unlikely hit was cheese-flavored chocolate. Some high-end chocolatiers in Tokyo sell chocolates containing foie gras.

Chocolate Cheese

Just when you thought you'd seen it all, a New Zealand dairy company released chocolate-flavored cheese slices in Taiwan in 2005. Six months later, the company was experiencing so much success, having garnered 10 percent of the cheese market, that it decided to expand the product to Singapore, Malaysia, Indonesia and Thailand. I guess nothing beats processed cheese besides processed cheese and chocolate.

China, the Final Frontier

Asia is now considered by major chocolate manufacturers to be the final frontier and since 2005 has been aggressively pursued by major chocolate companies worldwide.

Of all the Asian countries, though, chocolate manufacturers are paying the closest attention to China, where chocolate is becoming more and more fashionable. Per capita chocolate consumption in China is still much lower than the world average, at less than two ounces of chocolate per person per year. China didn't even launch its first chocolate website until 2000, and even then, it was sponsored by chocolate giant Mars.

Even in Japan and South Korea, average per capita chocolate consumption is more than five pounds per year, much higher than that of China.

Compare that to Western Europe, where the average person consumes over 17 pounds per year, and consider China's population of more than 1.3. billion, and you can see why world chocolate makers are so keen.

Working against the trend, in October 2008, British candy maker Cadbury had to recall chocolate made in its Beijing factory after tens of thousands of Chinese children became ill. It was discovered that the chocolate contained the industrial chemical melamine.

Even so, all the extra efforts from chocolate companies have shown an increase in chocolate consumption of 25 percent a year in Asia and 30 percent in China. Chocolate is still very expensive in China, and less than one percent of those 1.3 billion people is buying chocolate; nonetheless, chocolate is making progress. A sure sign is that fake versions of famous chocolate brands are starting to appear in candy stores. Unfortunately, this is now creating concern that another problem will arise—there won't be enough chocolate. Some even predict that this will lead to global chocolate wars.

Shocklaid
in Manx Gaelic

A DARK SPORT COAT AND A PINK CRUSTACEAN

When using chocolate in a savory dish, think of it more as a spice than a main ingredient. Taste or flavor is actually more a matter of smell, and research has shown that up to 80 percent of what we think of as taste is perceived by our sense of smell.

I am exploring different ways to enjoy chocolate in a less-traditional sense, and this chocolate-covered shrimp recipe is just like the Jimmy Buffet album after which it was named—a romantic individualist, eccentric and drunk.

Ingredients

1 cup finest plain dark chocolate containing at least
  70 percent cocoa, chopped
1/2 cup milk
3 Tbsp extra virgin olive oil
2 garlic cloves, crushed
1 lb shrimp, peeled and deveined
salt to season
1 cup white wine
small bunch fresh parsley, chopped

Combine chocolate and milk in a double boiler and stir until melted.

Sauté garlic in olive oil in a medium-sized frying pan.

Add shrimp and cook until pink and opaque.

Add salt and wine and let reduce, then add parsley.

Plate and drizzle with melted chocolate. Serves four.

SWEET TALK

This chocolate-covered garlic recipe boasts a unique flavor combination that, if nothing else, will keep your guests talking. Light red wines such as Chianti or Cab work well in this recipe, but whatever decent red wine you have on hand can be used. Some chocolate does not melt well and may turn out lumpy, so be sure to use a good-quality baking chocolate.

As part of my Chocolate Focus Group, my friend Laura agreed to test out this recipe for me, which I found intriguing. I had a few bottles of red wine sitting around and offered to come over with one as a donation. We drank the entire bottle, forgetting to leave the half-cup needed for the recipe. The very next night, I came over with a second bottle. We drank the entire thing. Finally, Laura had to wait until the morning of the tasting to get the wine. The point of the story is that cooking is as much about socializing as it is about eating.

Ingredients
24 medium-sized garlic cloves
1/2 cup red wine
1/4 cup sugar
2-inch piece of lemon rind
2 oz bittersweet or semisweet Lindt or Baker's chocolate

Peel the garlic cloves and remove the root end. Discard any cloves that have brown spots, or cut the spots away.

Bring the garlic, wine, sugar and lemon rind to a simmer in a small, heavy saucepan.

Reduce the heat, cover and cook over low heat for 25 to 30 minutes, stirring occasionally.

THE LAST BITE: CHOCOLATE RECIPES

Test the garlic for tenderness with the point of a sharp knife. Cool the garlic cloves on a plate covered with a piece of wax paper. They will be very sticky.

Melt the chocolate in a double boiler over medium heat.

Cover another plate with a piece of wax paper. Insert a toothpick into a clove of garlic and hold it over the edge of the pan. With a small spoon, cover the clove lightly with melted chocolate. Place the coated clove on the wax paper to cool and harden. Coat the remaining cloves.

Store the chocolate-coated cloves in a covered container in a cool place. Do not refrigerate, or the chocolate will change color. These are best eaten within 24 to 48 hours.

WHITE CHOCOLATE TRASH

I think there is nothing better than mixing chocolate with something salty, a trend that has more recently been made famous by the sweet 'n' salty granola bar. This recipe is nothing new, but it's one of my favorites and a reliable standby. Called "trash," likely because of the variety of different ingredients in it, the recipe yields a large quantity, and the ingredients can easily be substituted with whatever you have in the house.

Poor white chocolate—it's the black sheep of the chocolate family. It can't even technically be called "chocolate." In a peculiar role reversal, white chocolate is the minority of the cocoa world. No matter. Whether or not white chocolate is "real," I don't see any need to discriminate.

Ingredients
2 lbs good-quality white chocolate
6 cups crispy rice cereal squares, e.g., Rice Chex
3 cups toasted oat cereal
2 cups thin pretzel sticks
2 cups cashews
12-oz package mini candy-coated chocolate pieces

Melt chocolate in a large saucepan over low heat or in a microwave until just until soft. Stir until melted.

Combine the crispy rice cereal squares, toasted oat cereal, pretzels, cashews and candy in a large bowl. Stir chocolate into mixture. Fold onto wax paper and let cool. Cut into pieces and serve.

SAUCY MINX

It is amazing who stepped up to the plate and came out of the woodwork to help me in the making of this book. It turns out that my hairdresser Heidi is an avid cook and lover of chocolate who enjoys making up recipes in what little spare time she has. The next three recipes are compliments of her. This Spicy Cocoa Steak Rub is a lot like Heidi— there's an edge and kick to her that you can't help but love.

Ingredients
3 Tbsp unsweetened cocoa powder
4 Tbsp instant espresso coffee
1/2 tsp cayenne pepper (more if you like it spicier)
1/2 tsp chili powder
1 tsp garlic powder
olive oil
6–8 medium-sized steaks

Mix the five first ingredients together in a bowl.

Lay steaks out in a pan and coat generously with olive oil.

Spoon mixture onto steaks. Rub into meat and let stand 30 minutes.

Barbecue the steaks and enjoy!

"And above all…think chocolate!"
–Betty Crocker

DIRTY LITTLE SECRET

The "dirty little secret" in this crunchy brie panini with chocolate soup is the alcohol.

Never one to shy away from any type of libation, I love a cocktail disguised as a lunchtime meal. The combination of crunchy bread, warm, melted cheese and bittersweet chocolate is a satisfying indulgence sure to cure even the foulest of tempers. If your tastes run a little sweeter, use milk chocolate in the recipe. For a more intense hit, try the bittersweet.

Ingredients
1 cup 2% milk
1 cup heavy cream
1 cup good-quality bittersweet or milk chocolate, cut
    into chunks
1/4 cup Frangelico or liqueur of your choice
1 Tbsp honey
1/2 wheel of Brie, thinly sliced
8 slices of baguette with flaky crust, cut about 1/2 to
    3/4 inch thick
4 Tbsp room-temperature unsalted butter

Combine the milk and cream in a medium saucepan and bring to a simmer over medium heat. Add chocolate and whisk constantly until smooth, about four minutes. Remove from heat, add the liqueur. (If you are making this with the kids, be sure to leave this step out!) Cover to keep warm.

Place the sliced Brie onto four slices of bread and top with the remaining bread. Spread 1 1/2 teaspoons of butter on each side of the sandwich.

Grill each sandwich in a panini press if you have one. If not, heat a medium skillet over medium-high heat. Grill each sandwich separately until golden brown, pressing down with a spatula, approximately one to two minutes each side.

Ladle the chocolate soup into four shallow bowls and serve immediately with one sandwich each.

BREAKFAST IN BED

My motto: "If you want breakfast in bed, then sleep in the kitchen." But Heidi's chocolate pancakes with blood orange sauce are worth getting out of bed for. They are even more decadent if you can cajole and coax your sweetie into preparing them for you. I try to incorporate chocolate into every meal of the day. The perfect Sunday morning treat, I swear these taste better in your pajamas.

Pancakes:
Ingredients
2 eggs
3 Tbsp sour cream
2 cups milk
1 tsp vanilla
3 Tbsp sugar
1 1/2 cups all-purpose flour
3 Tbsp unsweetened cocoa powder
1/4 tsp salt
2 tsp baking powder
2 Tbsp melted butter

Beat eggs, sour cream, milk and vanilla together. In a separate bowl, sift together sugar, flour, cocoa powder, salt and baking powder. Add flour mixture to liquid with a whisk. Fold in melted butter.

Heat a skillet with butter and add the pancake mixture, forming each into a circle about 3 inches in diameter. Flip the pancakes once bubbles have formed in the center.

Blood Orange Sauce:
Ingredients
3 Tbsp butter
4 Tbsp brown sugar
3 blood oranges, peeled
1/2 tsp vanilla

Melt butter in a skillet. Add brown sugar and simmer for
5 minutes. Squeeze the juice from two of the blood oranges
and add to the pan. Let simmer one minute.

Slice the remaining orange into three sections, removing the
segments. Add the orange pieces to the skillet and let warm
thoroughly. Add vanilla, stir and remove from heat. If sauce
is too thick, add 2 tablespoons of water.

Assemble plate. Stack three pancakes and drizzle with blood
orange sauce. Serve with a dollop of whipped cream, and
garnish with almond slices and shaved semisweet chocolate.

BETWEEN THE SHEETS

This boozy hot chocolate from my friend, Pamela, is a Christmastime favorite that solidified our friendship. Great for drinking while decorating the tree, warming you up on a cold winter's night or getting you through the workday (just kidding), this drink is not for the faint of heart. One cup will have you convinced that you are a master decorator, prima ballerina or Don Juan. It will most definitely help you slow down and stop worrying about that long list of things that need to get done. If you've been nice all year, now's your chance to make up for it.*

Ingredients
1/2 cup semisweet, milk or mint chocolate shavings
1 cup whole milk
1/2 oz Frangelico
1/2 oz Amaretto
1/2 oz Irish cream
1/2 oz white chocolate liqueur
whipped cream and chocolate shavings to top

In a medium saucepan, heat milk over medium heat. Add the chocolate shavings and stir. Remove pan from heat.

Combine the alcohol in your favorite mug and pour the hot chocolate into the mug. Top with whipped cream and sprinkle with chocolate shavings and serve. Double, triple or quadruple the recipe depending on the size of your anxiety and/or party.

*Do not attempt to operate any heavy machinery after consuming this beverage. Fireplace and cute boyfriend recommended, but certainly not necessary.

MOM'S TURTLE SQUARES

When my siblings and I go home for Christmas, we are each allowed to choose one favorite dessert recipe. I always pick the Turtle squares. Although my mother has 50 years' worth of recipes, I chose this one because it's so quick, easy and delicious that even I could make it at home. Not that I would ever do that.

Ingredients

1 14-oz package of caramel squares
1 can sweetened condensed milk
1 box German chocolate cake mix
1 cup chocolate chips
1 cup pecans, chopped
3/4 cup butter

Preheat oven to 350°F.

Prepare the German chocolate cake mix according to package directions and mix with 3/4 cup sweetened condensed milk and 3/4 cup butter.

Spread half the cake mixture into a greased 9x13x2-inch pan. It is important to use this size of pan, otherwise the squares will be too thick and "cakey."

Bake at 350°F for 15 minutes.

Combine caramels and the remaining 1/4 cup sweetened condensed milk over low heat, stirring frequently.

Let cool. Pour caramel mixture over baked cake. Sprinkle on chocolate chips. Sprinkle pecans over the top.

Cover with remaining cake mix (Mom's tip: the mixture is quite often stiff, so put the cake mix in the microwave for 30 seconds to make it easier to cover the fillings.)

Bake at 350°F for 20 to 25 minutes or until mixture is still fairly soft but cooked through.

Let cool and serve.

TALL, DARK AND HANDSOME

Originally a Jean Paré favorite, this sweet treat was named "Six in a Pan," presumably for the six different layers in the dessert. Whether through intention or mistake, the name somehow evolved to become "Sex in a Pan." Although it's possibly because a lot of people found it to be a truly decadent dessert, I think that it could stand to be even a little more sinful.

A small-town favorite for years, it is time to bring "Six in a Pan" into the 21st century, jazz it up and, for goodness sakes, get rid of that awful pan.

Ingredients
1 cup flour
1/2 cup butter, softened
3/4 cup chopped pecans or ground almonds
1 1/2 quarts each of gourmet chocolate fudge brownie ice cream and vanilla Swiss almond ice cream, softened.
1/2 container (6 oz) frozen whipped topping, thawed
1 1/2 cup malted milk balls (or toffee pieces, sponge pieces or candy of your choice, crushed)
8 hazelnut wafer rolls
8 champagne flutes

Combine flour, butter and pecans and press into a 9x13x2-inch baking pan or CorningWare dish. Bake at 350°F for 25 minutes until lightly brown.

Spoon approximately 2 tablespoons of the crumb mixture into the bottom of 8 champagne flutes. You can choose either to let the mixture cool, or serve it straight from the oven, but I prefer the contrast of the warm, crumbly mixture with the cold ice cream.

Spoon in approximately the same quantity of vanilla Swiss almond ice cream into each flute glass.

Place the malted milk balls or other candy in a sealable plastic sandwich bag and crush with a rolling pin or meat mallet until the candy is in coarse pieces. Reserve 1/3 cup.

Cream whipped topping and crushed candy pieces together. Add approximately 1 tablespoon to each of the champagne flutes.

Add 2 tablespoons of chocolate fudge brownie ice cream to the next layer and more of the whipped cream mixture.

Sprinkle with remaining crushed candy pieces and serve with hazelnut wafer rolls.

PILLOW BOOK

A pillow book is typically a collection of notes that reflect a period of someone's life. A personal journal of observations or musings, a pillow book has a sultry, intimate connotation to it that I find irresistible. Some years ago, a movie was made in which a translator, played by actor Ewan McGregor, uses the body of his female lover and writes his own pillow book on her flesh. This sensual and suggestive movie befits the name of this equally alluring chocolate cake. This recipe is labor intensive and a bit finicky, but as with any lover, the patience, attention and doting will pay dividends you never thought possible.

Ganache Center:
Ingredients
2/3 cup whipping cream
1/4 cup water
1/4 cup ground coffee
4 oz bittersweet chocolate, coarsely chopped
3 Tbsp unsalted butter, softened

In a small saucepan, combine whipping cream, water and ground coffee. Heat over medium heat until hot. Remove from heat and let stand 15 minutes. Strain the mixture through a fine sieve into a clean one-quart saucepan. Heat mixture again over medium heat and bring just to a boil. Remove from heat.

Add butter and chocolate to cream mixture and mix until melted together. Line a 9x9-inch square baking pan with aluminum foil, letting foil extend over two sides. Pour ganache into pan. Freeze until firm, about 1 hour.*

Cookie Batter:
Ingredients
1/3 cup almond meal
3 large eggs, separated
Pinch of salt
3/4 cup sugar
6 Tbsp unsalted butter, melted
8 oz bittersweet chocolate, melted
1/3 cup uncooked Cream of Wheat
1/4 cup toasted cocoa nibs (cocoa beans broken into small
    pieces and finely chopped), optional

Spray eight 3 1/2-inch ramekins with cooking spray. Line
bottoms with parchment circles and spray again.

In a medium skillet over medium heat, cook almond meal
until lightly toasted and fragrant, stirring frequently, about
5 minutes. Turn meal onto a plate to cool.*

In a medium bowl, add 3 egg whites and salt and beat with
an electric mixer on medium-high speed until soft peaks
begin to form. Shift mixer to high and gradually beat in
sugar until whites stiffen.

In a large bowl, combine almond meal, 3 egg yolks, butter,
chocolate, Cream of Wheat and cocoa nibs, and stir until
blended. Fold in egg white mixture. Spoon mixture into
a large food storage bag, and snip a large hole in one corner.
Pipe mixture into bottom of ramekins to cover, about
1/2 inch thick.

Remove ganache from the freezer, lifting it from the pan
using the foil ends. With a 2 1/4-inch round cutter, cut out
eight circles. Reserve the remaining ganache pieces. Place a
circle in the center of each ramekin. Pipe remaining batter
over and around ganache to cover. Smooth tops. Freeze until
firm, about one hour.

BETTER-THAN-BRAD-PITT BROWNIES

With a name like this, one can't help but be curious about the decadence of a brownie that could rival the likes of Brad Pitt. Could there possibly be such a thing? Delightfully, it turns out to be true! These brownies get their amazing texture by being baked for a short period of time and then chilled in the refrigerator.

A masterpiece creation of New York City pastry chef Ayse Dizioglu of the famed Polka Dot Cake Studio, this is one of the few recipes that has not been changed. It is perfection.

Before Chef Dizioglu so generously donated the recipe to the project, I momentarily thought I might need to change the name or part of the recipe, which would have been tragic. "Yummier-than-Yanni" just doesn't quite cut it.

If you only make one recipe from this book, this should be it. If you don't have a Valentine's date, fear not—you have the Better-Than-Brad-Pitt Brownie, which is so good it'll make you forget that there ever even was an Angelina.

Ingredients
14 oz unsweetened or bittersweet chocolate, chopped
1/4 cup cocoa powder
12 oz (1 1/2 cups) butter, softened
3 cups granulated sugar (if you use bittersweet chocolate, use
    only 2 1/2 cups sugar)
1 tsp salt
6 eggs, at room temperature
2 cups all purpose flour, sifted
1 3/4 cups chocolate morsels
1 cup walnuts

Preheat oven to 300°F.

Butter a 9x13x2-inch pan and line the bottom with parchment. If you aren't baking for a large quantity of people, it is recommended that you halve the recipe and use a square 8 1/2x8 1/2-inch pan. It will make more than enough to satisfy your craving.

Melt the chocolate and cocoa powder together in a double boiler or in the microwave in 5-second intervals.

Cream the butter, sugar, and salt for 2 minutes until fluffy. Add the eggs, one at a time, mixing well between each addition and scraping the bowl down.

Add the melted chocolate and mix until the color is even.

Add the flour in three additions, mixing gently. When all the flour is incorporated, fold in the chocolate morsels and walnuts and mix well.

Pour into the prepared pan and spread the batter evenly. Bake for 25 to 30 minutes. The top will look set and papery, the middle will feel very soft, and the edges will have just started to pull away from the sides of the pan. Do not over-bake.

Cool the brownies on a cooling rack on the counter until completely cool, about 1 to 2 hours. Then chill the brownies in the refrigerator for 4 to 6 hours. The chilling is the most important part as it sets the fudge-like texture.

Cut brownies into small pieces because they are very rich.

MR. RIGHT

A new wave in eating is the raw food lifestyle. Raw foodists believe that fruits, leafy greens, vegetables, sprouts, nuts and seeds contain vital, restorative enzymes that are destroyed by cooking. The cacao nut is the most widely consumed nut in the world, and yet is seldom used as such in North America.

This handmade, homemade, raw chocolate recipe is compliments of Malcolm Saunders, a raw chocolatier and superfood chef who specializes in teaching others the alchemy of raw organic chocolate and superfood plant-based cuisine.

Malcolm believes that the cacao bean is much more powerful if you preserve the integrity of its nutrients by not roasting it. He also believes that it is possible for you to make the most delicious, handmade chocolate in your own home. So if you don't happen to have a Mr. Right, this delicious chocolate is a perfect Mr. Right Now.

Ingredients
1 cup cacao butter or coconut oil, melted in a double boiler
1/2 cup cacao powder
1/4 cup carob or mesquite powder*
1/4 cup dark agave syrup or nectar*
1 vanilla bean with the seeds scraped out

Mix ingredients together in a bowl and pour onto cookie sheet or other lined or non-stick tray or pan. Place pan in fridge or freezer to chill. Eat as is.

*Note: Agave is a natural sweetener commercially produced in Mexico. Fermented agave is the main ingredient in tequila, but in this natural form, it is an innocuous sweetener, much like honey. Carob, mesquite powder and agave can all be found at a growing number of health-food stores.

ABOUT THE AUTHOR & ILLUSTRATOR

KAREN ROWE

Karen Rowe has had a life long passion for three things: writing, traveling and chocolate. A self-proclaimed professional hedonist and former teacher, she has spent time volunteering, teaching and exploring in France, Korea, Mexico, Guatemala and, most recently, Belize. Karen has written for *The New West Online*, *Opulence Magazine* and *Calgary Herald's Q Blog* and currently lives in Calgary, Alberta. She has never met a chocolate she didn't like.

ROGER GARCIA

Roger Garcia is a self-taught artist with some formal training who specializes in cartooning and illustration. He is an immigrant from El Salvador, and during the last few years, his work has been primarily cartoons and editorial illustrations in pen and ink. Recently he has started painting once more. Focusing on simplifying the human form, he uses a bright minimal palette and as few elements as possible. His work can be seen in newspapers, magazines, promo material and on www.rogergarcia.ca.